SOFTWARE ARCHITECTURE AND DECISION-MAKING

SOFTWARE ARCHITECTURE AND DECISION-MAKING

LEVERAGING LEADERSHIP, TECHNOLOGY, AND PRODUCT MANAGEMENT TO BUILD GREAT PRODUCTS

Srinath Perera

✦ Addison-Wesley

For information about buying this title in bulk quantities, or for special sales opportunities (which may include electronic versions; custom cover designs; and content particular to your business, training goals, marketing focus, or branding interests), please contact our corporate sales department at corpsales@pearsoned.com or (800) 382-3419.

For government sales inquiries, please contact governmentsales@pearsoned.com.

For questions about sales outside the U.S., please contact intlcs@pearson.com.

Visit us on the Web: informit.com/aw

Library of Congress Control Number: 2023946912

Copyright © 2024 Pearson Education, Inc.

Hoboken, NJ

Cover image: wowomnom/Shutterstock; AVA AVA/Shutterstock

ISBN-13: 978-0-13-824973-1
ISBN-10: 0-13-824973-3

1 2023

Pearson's Commitment to Diversity, Equity, and Inclusion

Pearson is dedicated to creating bias-free content that reflects the diversity of all learners. We embrace the many dimensions of diversity, including but not limited to race, ethnicity, gender, socioeconomic status, ability, age, sexual orientation, and religious or political beliefs.

Education is a powerful force for equity and change in our world. It has the potential to deliver opportunities that improve lives and enable economic mobility. As we work with authors to create content for every product and service, we acknowledge our responsibility to demonstrate inclusivity and incorporate diverse scholarship so that everyone can achieve their potential through learning. As the world's leading learning company, we have a duty to help drive change and live up to our purpose to help more people create a better life for themselves and to create a better world.

Our ambition is to purposefully contribute to a world where:

- Everyone has an equitable and lifelong opportunity to succeed through learning.
- Our educational products and services are inclusive and represent the rich diversity of learners.
- Our educational content accurately reflects the histories and experiences of the learners we serve.
- Our educational content prompts deeper discussions with learners and motivates them to expand their own learning (and worldview).

While we work hard to present unbiased content, we want to hear from you about any concerns or needs with this Pearson product so that we can investigate and address them.

- Please contact us with concerns about any potential bias at https://www.pearson.com/report-bias.html.

This book is dedicated to my family: Miyuru, Basilu, and Nithika. Your presence brings color and purpose to my life. And to my parents, whose unwavering love and trust continue to astonish and uplift me.

I also extend my heartfelt gratitude to Frank for your steadfast support throughout this journey to its realization. Your insights were invaluable in shaping the core idea of this book.

Contents

About the Author

I started my architecting journey as an Apache open-source developer and have continued that for 20 years. I learned a lot by watching and later participating in architecture discussions in developer lists for those open-source projects, which is a great place for an aspiring architect to start.

I have played a major role in the architecture of Apache Axis2, Apache Airavata, WSO2 CEP (Siddhi), and WSO2 Choreo. I have designed two SOAP engines and worked closely with four. I was (and continue to be) a committer (a developer who can commit to a code base) for Apache Axis, Axis2, Apache Geronimo, and Apache Airavata.

I joined WSO2 in 2009. WSO2 products are used by many Fortune 500 companies such as airlines, banks, governments, and so on. At WSO2, I played an architecture review role for 10+ projects and 100+ releases. I reviewed hundreds of customer-solution architectures and deployments and sat in on thousands of architecture reviews.

At WSO2, when we faced a problem that could not be resolved by the immediate team, we set up a war room, where a hand-picked team restlessly attacked the problem. I have been in many war rooms and have led several, which have made me painfully aware of mistakes made in the software architecture. I've had a front row seat to world-class technical leadership and have also built many systems and learned from mistakes.

Later switching to analytics and AI-related topics, I co-designed WSO2 Siddhi and envisioned and shaped the AI features in WSO2 Choreo. Throughout this time, I published 40+ peer-reviewed research articles, which have been referenced by thousands of other research publications.

I hope you enjoy this book. Given the central role software plays in the world today, I will be content if this book helps make you a better software architect, knowing that I have contributed to better software that will be the lifeblood of the world for many years.

Register your copy of **Software Architecture and Decision-Making** on the InformIT site for convenient access to updates and/or corrections as they become available. To start the registration process, go to informit.com/register and log in or create an account. Enter the product ISBN (**9780138249731**) and click Submit. Look on the Registered Products tab for an Access Bonus Content link next to this product, and follow that link to access any available bonus materials. If you would like to be notified of exclusive offers on new editions and updates, please check the box to receive email from us.

Introduction to Software Leadership

When we are developing software systems, our goal is to build systems that meet quality standards and that provide the highest return on investment (ROI) in the long run or in a predefined time horizon. This, in turn, becomes the goal of software architecture, which is the blueprint for building software systems.

Here, ROI is not just about being economical. If spending more on the product results in more revenue, consider that a good ROI. On the other hand, shoddy design leads to numerous changes later, ultimately costing a lot more. Good software architecture balances both extremes and maximizes ROI.

Architectural design includes many things—for example, finding the right abstractions, deciding which features to include, determining the depth of each feature, setting quality of service (QOS) parameters, establishing the degree of flexibility, timing, and user experience.

Role of Judgment

As software architects, we learn about abstractions, architecture styles, and patterns. We study their pros and cons, which one to use in a given situation, and how to compose them with an awareness of pitfalls, negative examples, and use cases. However, many errors are made not because we do not understand these things. Most design mistakes are caused by a lack of judgment, not by a lack of knowledge.

Here, *judgment* refers to the ability to make considered decisions or arrive at sensible conclusions optimizing for the most important outcome.

I have seen this outcome again and again in my 20 years of architecting systems. Here are the common mistakes I've found:

- Trying to incorporate too many features required by the user's journey
- Making the design too flexible or too consistent, which impacts future changes
- Limiting depth, which significantly affects user experience (UX)
- Solving useless problems for the end user
- Inadequately focusing on the user's journey and experience
- Missing delivery timetables

We make most of these mistakes because we do not know about the future, about the users who will use the system, and about how the system works at the edge of its capabilities. Here, I see the need for judgment. I see leadership challenges, not technical challenges!

Let's explore what I mean by that.

To me, leadership is about managing uncertainty, bringing order to chaos, providing hope for a better future, and progressing toward that future. Consider the following:

> *A leader is a dealer in hope. —Napoleon Bonaparte*

This is not to say leaders must be omniscient and always know what the future will bring, but they should have a *vision* of the future; they should manage uncertainty in such a way that minimizes risk. Leaders should communicate their vision and its implementation to others and shepherd them toward that vision.

Let me repeat the same statement from an architect's point of view. It is not to say software architects must be omniscient and always know how a system will be used and what it should have, but they should have a vision of the overall solution. They should manage uncertainty in such a way that minimizes risk. Leaders should communicate their vision and implementation to the team and guide them toward building the system and then operating it.

I am not saying that knowledge is not important for an architect. It is. However, judgment plays a key role too. Sadly, knowledge is commonplace, whereas judgment is not.

I have seen a lot of good books and articles about software architectural concepts: Bob Martin's books, Gregor Hohpe's books, and Martin Fowler's blogs, to name a few. Yet, they focus mainly on knowledge and less on judgment.

I have also seen a lot of good books on leadership: *The Hard Things About Hard Things* by Ben Horowitz, *Trillion Dollar Coach* by Eric Schmidt et al., *Team of Teams: New Rules of Engagement for a Complex World* by Stanley McChrystal, *Good Strategy, Bad Strategy* by Richard Rumelt, and other books by Jocko Willink, to name a few. They discuss judgment but only at a general level, not at a technical level. There is a gap between good leadership and good software architectural judgment.

Goal of This Book

This book discusses the gap between the two—leadership and software architectural judgment. It describes software leadership and how we can use it to the best advantage when building our systems. As mentioned, my experience shows that many of our architectural mistakes come from the gap between knowledge and judgment.

This is not a book about how to manage your team, nor is it a book about engineering management or about HR and how to build the team. It's also not a book about strategy. Further, this book does not cover how to create a vision. You must have a vision—your own or one shared by your cofounders or executive board members. Although there is a lot written about vision, I am not sure it can be explained sufficiently.

This is a technical book, so it is a book about technical judgment. It explains principles and concepts I believe a senior architect must understand deeply and discusses how to employ those principles to manage uncertainty. This is a book about how technical leaders/architects should think and how to oversee their product by managing uncertainty.

For example, one thesis of this book is to *think deeply but implement slowly*. Another example is that leaders must define the scope, taking up the yoke of uncertainty without passing it down to coworkers. Questions and principles discussed in this book help us manage uncertainty and provide a framework for making decisions.

Is this book useful if you are not in charge? I think it is. People follow whoever offers to handle uncertainty in order to progress. Good architects start to play the role years before they are given the title. The more knowledgeable you are, the better chance you'll have if you do choose to lead. Take the initiative; help your leader and deliver. You will find you own more and more. Titles will follow.

If you believe someone plays that role better than you, by all means, follow, question, and learn from them! In this case, there is a lot you can do to help the leader, using what we discuss in the book. Your turn will follow.

This book draws examples from many role models who exemplify technical leadership. I name two specifically: Kelly Johnson, who designed aircraft like the U-2 and the Blackbird SR-71, and the Wright brothers, Orville and Wilbur, whom we all know. These leaders showed a kind of deep technical control that made systems that seemed to be impossible possible, while utilizing limited resources. Granted, there are many software leaders like Jeff Dean of Google, whom I hold in the same esteem, but they are contemporaries, and their methods are not yet published as books. This fact forces me to choose the previously mentioned models for the book.

As we all know, the Wright brothers built the first powered airplane with sustained and controlled flight. They had no college education and owned and operated a bicycle shop. They competed against well-funded professionals and yet went on to win. Granted, there were many aircraft designs before the Wright brothers, but they were the first to get all the parameters of the design right. The Wright brothers showed great judgment by building a glider, learning how to control it, learning to tweak it, and then adding propellers and engines, which gradually evolved their gilder into an aircraft. Figuring out the right parameters is a lesson we all can use. The Wright brothers had an intuitive feel to the design, which they acquired over the years. They later achieved both fame and fortune.

Kelly Johnson was the aircraft designer for the Lockheed U-2, the SR-71 Blackbird, and 40 other aircrafts. The Blackbird is invisible to radar, can outrun missiles, and has never been shot down in 20+ years of service. It was the first production aircraft to exceed Mach 3 (three times the speed of sound). Kelly also built the first fighter capable of Mach 2 and the first fighter to exceed 400 mph. His U-2 craft reached and sustained altitudes of 70,000 feet.[1] He could take an impossible goal, break it into doable tasks, demand excellence, and then make everything work. Kelly was known to finish projects early and under budget, returning money to the government. His boss reportedly said, "That damned Swede can actually see air," referring to Kelly's intuitive feel to the design.[2]

The terms *architecture* and *design* are often used interchangeably, although design is a full detailed blueprint (e.g., class diagrams and sequence diagrams), whereas architecture is the high-level conceptual view (e.g., component view and component-level sequence diagram). We focus on the high-level view; hence, I use the term *architecture* throughout.

We can use the three layers of architecture of The Open Group Architecture Framework (TOGAF) to pinpoint topics we focus on in this book:

- The business architecture layer sketches out the business operations and shows how various components work together to propel the business's workings.

- The information systems architecture layer splits into two parts: data and application architecture. Data architecture centers around categorizing different data types and highlighting their connections. On the other hand, application architecture identifies unique system parts, such as services, and clarifies their interaction within the system.

- The technology architecture layer describes the specifically chosen technologies. They include elements like software standards, software packages used, hardware, networks, and the fine details of security.

The core focus of this book rests on the information system architecture. Nonetheless, we may discuss technology architecture if the choice of technology significantly impacts our discussion.

The connection between business architecture and information system architecture is more intricate. The design of the information system architecture heavily depends on various business considerations. These factors include not only the business architecture but also elements like project schedules, the skills of the team, and the challenges from competitors. Although these considerations are not usually included in the business architecture in

---

1. https://en.wikipedia.org/wiki/Lockheed_U-2

2. https://en.wikipedia.org/wiki/Kelly_Johnson_(engineer)

frameworks like TOGAF, they do influence the implementation of the architecture and the strategic course of the organization. Together, these are referred to as the "business context." A main challenge in system architecture is to keep this business context in mind when making technology decisions. Ensuring this is a responsibility that falls to leadership. A key goal of the five questions we discuss in this book is to ensure we maintain this business context.

There are two prominent approaches to system architecture:

- Waterfall

- Agile

The *waterfall* approach is based on the premise that it's feasible to identify the system's requirements in full detail beforehand. Therefore, this approach suggests thorough planning followed by execution. An example of this approach can be seen in the TOGAF architecture design model (ADM), which demonstrates how to capture requirements accurately and develop them. In addition, groups like the Object Management Group (OMG) and International Organization for Standardization (ISO) offer standards supporting similar conceptual models.

On the other hand, iterative approaches, like *agile*, focus on quickly rolling out a version and collaborating with users to refine requirements and construct a system that can genuinely benefit the user.

When pitting these two approaches against each other, I lean toward agile. Efforts have been made to blend iterative features with models like ADM, but in practice, it's often too complicated to maintain the rapid pace needed for iterative models (usually one- to two-week iterations). With large organizations and complex projects, more central planning could be justified, though, even after working with hundreds of enterprise companies, including Fortune 500 firms, I have yet to see such a project deliver exceptional results.

Many software processes, such as TOGAF ADM, standards, and reference architectures, are grounded in the waterfall model and aim to capture the requirements precisely. While valuable lessons can be learned from TOGAF, OMG, and ISO, they operate under the assumption that requirements can be largely defined beforehand and will only undergo gradual changes. In contrast, I believe our experiences have proven otherwise. I endorse a more interactive or agile approach where requirements are kept simpler and informal, continuously improving in short iterations, while learning from users.

At a broader design level, I favor breaking the system into loosely connected subsystems (each potentially interacting with users and providing value), defining APIs between them, and then operating them independently with high-level oversight to connect the dots.

While architects may find utility in TOGAF and similar models, I hesitate to recommend them in this book. This is an opinion formed from my experiences.

The focus of this book is on agile approaches. So, before we dive into the book, it is useful to understand the typical roles in a software project. Product managers, with the help of business stakeholders, UX designers, and architects, decide what to build. Architects work with engineering managers and the team to build the product. The product manager then works with everyone to ensure the required quality (demanding excellence).

The scope of the architect's role might change, based on where the work takes place. For example, in a startup, architects might handle product management, deciding the features to build, whereas in a large company, architects might be disconnected from the requirement specifications. However, in an era when we are moving away from the waterfall approach to the iterative, agile software development approach, responsibilities are being shared, and these roles are merging. For example, I believe architects should work hand in hand with product managers when deciding which features to include, when to include them, and when defining UX, demanding excellence from the team.

This book is segmented into four parts. Although the book focuses on judgment, knowledge is just as important. Parts II and III delve into the topic of knowledge, while exploring how we can judge its use.

Part I: Introduction

In Part I, Chapter 2 discusses software architecture, uncertainty, and judgment. It identifies five questions and seven principles to help us handle uncertainty:

The five questions are

> When is the best time to market?
>
> What is the skill level of the team?
>
> What is our system's performance sensitivity?
>
> When can we rewrite the system?
>
> What are the hard problems?

The seven principles are

> Drive everything from the user's journey.
>
> Use an iterative thin slice strategy.
>
> On each iteration, add the most value for the least effort to support more users.
>
> Make decisions and absorb the risks.
>
> Design deeply things that are hard to change but implement them slowly.
>
> Eliminate the unknowns and learn from the evidence by working on hard problems early and in parallel.
>
> Understand the trade-offs between coherence and flexibility in the software architecture.

As we explore in detail in Chapter 2, these five questions and seven principles address each of the common architectural mistakes we often make.

Part II: Essential Background

In Part II, we dig into two performance and user experience (UX) areas, which, in my opinion, are not well understood by many architects. First is system performance, which decides what is and what is not feasible in our architectures. The second is UX, which often decides user adoption—thus, the system's destiny.

Chapter 3 is more detailed and technical compared to the other chapters. These specifics are crucial, and they aren't widely covered in other books. If you're initially seeking a broader understanding, you could briefly go through Chapter 3, but I recommend revisiting it to grasp the finer points eventually.

Chapter 4 emphasizes the importance of UX principles and persuades you to bring UX expertise into the team early on and listen to those experts' advice. Additionally, I want to stress the importance of UX for APIs, configurations, and extensions.

Part III: System Design

Part III focuses on how to build a system or an application. We discuss two levels: the macro level, where we compose services into a coherent architecture, and the micro level, where we learn how to build good services.

In this part, whenever possible, we explain a default architectural choice that works most of the time and more complex ones, discussing how to choose the right one for your company. This discussion includes anti-patterns and common mistakes. It talks about these technical ideas that I believe are critical:

Understanding macro architecture is described in

Chapter 5: Introduction

Chapter 6: Coordination

Chapter 7: Preserving Consistency of State

Chapter 8: Handling Security

Chapter 9: Handling HA and Scale

Chapter 10: Microservices Considerations

Writing a good usable service is described in Chapter 11.

Building stable systems is described in Chapter 12.

I dedicate a separate chapter to microservices considerations, instead of dispersing them in Chapters 6, 7, and 8. I believe this approach makes it easier to grasp the whole concept as a combined entity rather than understanding the parts separately.

I explain each technical decision based on the applicable five questions and seven principles.

Part IV: Putting Everything Together

Part IV includes only Chapter 13, which discusses how everything comes together. This chapter focuses on establishing a fast feedback cycle, removing anything that slows developers down from completing iterations, receiving feedback, and learning. This chapter urges leaders to ensure developers can do their jobs efficiently, while getting personally involved to solve any issues that hold the developers back.

2

Understanding Systems, Design, and Architecture

What Is Software Architecture?

Software architecture is a plan to build a software system. This plan usually involves two things: defining a system as a set of components and specifying how those components work together. In complex systems, this decomposition happens recursively, where the architect breaks down each component into smaller components and defines their behaviors.

There are good plans and bad plans. The same goes for software architecture. What are the goals of good software architecture?

The overarching goal of software systems (hence, for software architecture) is to build systems that meet quality standards and that provide the highest return on investment (ROI) in the long run or within a defined period of time. *Long run* is the operative ideal here. For example, if we do not invest long term and build a crappy product, we end up with unhappy users, ultimately losing their revenue or spending too much money trying to make them happy. Cheaper in the short run is often more expensive in the long run. You pay now, or you pay later. On the other hand, adding a critical new feature, thus spending more money, can give us more revenue, improving the ROI.

Three kinds of uncertainty complicate architecting. First, we have a partial understanding of our users and what they want. Second, we have a limited comprehension of how our systems behave, especially in complicated and new situations. Third, we fail to recognize that as use cases and users evolve, their requirements change. Therefore, we want our architectures to be easy to understand and flexible, enabling us to handle surprises.

When reaching for the best architecture, we can employ several best practices or tactics:

- Making decisions as late as possible. For example, when we start the design, we know the least about a system and the problems we are supposed to solve. If we can postpone solving some problems, we have an opportunity to learn more. This approach lets us make better design decisions.

- Envisioning a design that is easy to understand and to change. Problems change over time, and we may face a few surprises. Because a system goes through frequent changes over its lifetime, good architecture makes those changes easier.

- Saying no to features as much as possible. Many system features are rarely used, although they were often deemed important at design time. Knowing the audience, implementing only necessary features, and communicating why not may save us money in the long run.

Many argue that these tactics are always good, even considering them to be goals of the architecture. I disagree. To me, even those tactics incur costs; thus, everything is relative, and these tactics are useful only if they help us achieve the overarching goal. Let's look at a few examples.

If we know that a use case will significantly change in the future, forcing us to rewrite the system from scratch, we should not invest in making the current design extensible.

When writing a cloud app, we have two choices: We can choose a single cloud, taking advantage of its unique strengths for our application, or we can make the application portable across several cloud providers. Choosing only one cloud vendor makes development easier, but there is a chance that we may have to rewrite the system or parts of the system if porting to a different cloud. The cost of making the current version portable may be much higher than rewriting it, only if required.

You may have a great architecture that makes the system easy to change; however, it involves complicated concepts that will be hard for the current team to handle. (It may have been an adverse call forcing us to choose this architecture.) You fight with the army you have, at least until you have resources to enlist a better army.

You may be a startup trying to get your MVP out. Then, chances are you will rewrite everything once you are successful. You would not care for scale or even ease of change at this stage.

Uncertainties create risks, but the remedies have their costs too, which also create risks. Architecting is balancing those risks. Context is king, and it is hard to architect with evergreen rules and to get them right. To quote a *Star Trek: Discovery* episode:

> *Universal law is for lackeys. Context is for kings.*

Understanding all types of risks, planning around those uncertainties, communicating the plan, enlisting people, and managing risk along the way define *leadership*. This book discusses the leadership process in software architecting.

How to Design a System

As discussed, design requires holistic decisions that keep the big picture and final goal in focus. Although there are many good tactics such as creating designs that are easy to change, we need to ensure the medicine is not worse than the problem. Gregor Hohpe explains that architecture creates options, just like financing alternatives, which is an apt analogy because having options also incurs costs. Sometimes, it makes sense to have options, and sometimes it does not. An architect must have options and the wisdom to recognize when not to use them.

System design is like war: You must know your enemy (the problem, how often it changes, etc.) and your strengths and weaknesses of the team and yourself. Also, you must play the odds. For example, if the cost of being portable is 50% more, but there is only a 10% chance that you will have to move to a different cloud, then the expected cost of being portable early is 150%. However, if we choose to not be portable, then there is a 10% chance that we will have to port later. Let's assume that to port later we have to do 250% more work. Then, the expected cost of not being portable is (100% + 250 * 10%) = 125%, which suggests that we should go with the nonportable choice.

Chapter 1 discussed the concept of business context, which includes not only TOGAF's business architecture but also other factors like project timelines, team skills, and competitive threats. It's this business context along with user experience that add complexity to software architecture. Any given situation will present various trade-offs in terms of costs, which could include time, complexity, required skills, and benefits like performance, stability, and speed to market. The relative importance of these costs and benefits varies depending on the business context and user experience. Making these trade-offs and arriving at the right technical decision require sound judgment.

This book proposes five questions and seven principles that help us understand the context, acting as guideposts for good judgment. Part II and Part III discuss knowledge and explain how it relates to judgment.

As a reminder, the five questions include

- When is the best time to market?
- What is the skill level of the team?
- What is our system's performance sensitivity?
- When can we rewrite the system?
- What are the hard problems?

The seven principles are

- Drive everything from the user's journey.
- Use an iterative thin slice strategy.
- On each iteration, add the most value for the least effort to support more users.
- Make decisions and absorb the risks.
- Design deeply things that are hard to change but implement them slowly.
- Eliminate the unknowns and learn from the evidence by working on hard problems early and in parallel.
- Understand the trade-offs between cohesion and flexibility in the software architecture.

The five questions are designed to help us understand the terrain (or the business context). Starting with time, team, and performance requirements, the effects of the first two questions are well understood. Performance comes next because it determines how much precision we need in the design. Many find the fourth question regarding rewrites odd, but I believe there is a natural second phase to all projects, where we can rewrite the system. This question is crucial because it defines the first phase and lets us defer some hard but not immediate problems uncovered by the fifth question to the second phase. I believe this question significantly clarifies our scope.

Once we understand the terrain, the seven principles are about what to implement, when, and how. The first principle tells us we should look at everything from the vantage point of the user and choose only things that are useful for their journey. The second and third principles say that we should iterate, starting with a thin slide, exploring the design space, and getting user feedback. Next is the most important takeaway, making decisions and absorbing the risks. The fifth and sixth principles are about going into depth, and the seventh principle reminds us that most good architectural practices come with a cost, and this principle balances advantages and costs.

Five Questions

Good questions make us think, uncover details, and transform our understanding. I have found them to be a great tool when designing. These questions have helped me scope a system and dig into it. They are designed to ground us in concrete situations and to avoid grasping for ideals that often cause projects to fail.

Question 1: When Is the Best Time to Market?

The business, not the architect, decides the project timing. However, this is the first question that we, as architects, need to ask. Time can be our enemy because, often, even skills and money can't change the timeline of the product.

Time to market is everything, and our designs must incorporate these realities. When the deadlines are strict, we can design with the knowledge that we will be able to rewrite the system beyond the deadline.

My usual experience is that although the time-to-market deadlines are often not negotiable, features that should go into that version are often flexible. My recommendation is to work with a UX designer and product manager to understand the minimal features you must incorporate into the design and do it as fast as possible, using the most straightforward approach.

Question 2: What Is the Skill Level of the Team?

Leadership is about working with your team. Some teams are so good they might handle the system without any help from you at all. However, leadership is needed when we work with less-than-perfect teams.

> *You go to war with the army you have, not the army you might want or wish to have at a later time.*
> *—Donald Rumsfeld*

Take a hard, realistic look at your team. Your team may be veteran superstars, handpicked and employed by you over the years, fresh hires, or some mix of these. You must pick an architecture your team can manage. For example, do not pick an event-driven architecture or CQRS (Command and Query Responsibility Segregation)-based server unless you have a few people who have done this before. Those kinds of architectures have high costs in understandability and debugging challenges, and they most likely will cost much more in the long run unless the team understands their finer details.

What if you feel in your gut that CQRS is the right solution, but you do not have experts on board to achieve that architecture? I recommend designing the current version using a simple architecture and starting a proof of concept (PoC). That way, you can try out the CQRS in the background with the person who is most likely to handle it and with the hope that, in the second version, you will undertake CQRS.

You might be thinking, "Can't I train the team?" Yes, in some cases. For example, you might hire an expert who works shoulder to shoulder with the team for a few months. However, a deeper understanding of most complex systems takes time. My experience is giving someone a fingertip feel for performance, keeping in mind that the ability to handle details like concurrency or an LMAX disrupter takes at least a year, maybe two.[1]

Similarly, you should pick the programming language also based on the team. Programmers have many skills acquired around a given programming language, and it is often tough to change.

---

1. https://lmax-exchange.github.io/disruptor/

Certain abilities, like security and user experience, are essential. So, the leader must find a way to cover these areas. Doing so could involve hiring a consultant or the leader personally stepping in to support the team and provide guidance.

Rarely, the right choice could be to refuse to build certain software with a novice team. Instead, sometimes (in a startup, for instance) you can build a limited version (e.g., that scales less), which can then be used to justify more investment later. Even then, you need to make things very clear for people who are making the investment and make sure they know the risks.

Question 3: What Is Our System's Performance Sensitivity?

If a system operates close to the performance limits of a naive architecture, we say that the system is *performance sensitive*. Architectural considerations change significantly between systems that are sensitive and insensitive to performance.

The performance sensitivity of the system tells how much leeway you have and how much precision you need. Achieving a higher precision is like walking a tightrope; it is exponentially hard and needs experienced developers. Thus, performance-sensitive systems need exotic techniques, careful design, greater creativity, continuous performance measurements, and a feedback cycle. We need to test and identify unknowns through experiments as soon as possible. We must have a thin slice working end to end and invest early on in the system to collect detailed metrics on its mechanics. We discuss this style of design in Chapter 3. All this adds complexity and cost.

We can design performance-insensitive systems using a fingertip feel for the performance and simple architectural choices. We discuss this approach in detail in Chapter 3. Hence, the answer to this question significantly affects our architectural choices.

Note that many systems are performance insensitive. For example, using open-source service frameworks such as a Spring Boot and a database, you can easily implement a service that handles a few hundred requests per second. Even 50 requests per second are 4.32 million requests per day. With most businesses, if you are getting that many requests, chances are that you are already successful and can afford to write the second and third versions of the system. Most systems never need to exceed this limit.

Here's a second follow-up question: When we go beyond the limit of trivial implementation (e.g., 50 requests per second), will we have enough money to rewrite the system? Always ask this question: If we have that many requests, will we have enough money to rewrite the system? If the answer is yes, you can start with a simpler design and wait.

A much trickier scenario is if use cases require operating with latency bounds. We discuss this topic in Chapter 3. However, naive architecture can support (in most cases) expectations of latency of less than a few seconds (e.g., 1–10 seconds).

Question 4: When Can We Rewrite the System?

The fourth question helps us accept that we will rewrite the system eventually. For example, if you are a startup, do not try to build the architecture that you will need when you have a few billion users and hundreds of millions of dollars in revenue. When you get there, you will have enough money to rewrite the system several times over. Most successful systems have been rewritten many times over.

The common objection is that it would waste money to redo the system. Yes, it will cost, but to believe that you can think through all the details of a system as it will be in three to five years down the line is arrogance. There is so much uncertainty along the way. Chances are your system will not work for the first few moderate trials and will take longer to deliver.

Instead, be humble. Make the system work for the first 10,000 to 50,000 users, learn from them, and rewrite when the time is appropriate. Often, that time is not that far into the future. This approach helps us to be lean and simple, focusing on a few key problems, yet solving those systems properly. Do Things that Don't Scale!!.

Also, with the new IDEs, it is comparatively easy to refactor and redesign logic into a new structure. My belief is that we should plan to rewrite beyond key milestones (e.g., startup PoC to first serious funding round or beyond a million users). Having accepted that we will rewrite, we often realize that many features or guarantees can be done in the next rewrite.

Question 5: What Are the Hard Problems?

With the line of thinking I am proposing, it is easy to forget hard problems or push them out to the future. This question guards against such procrastination. But, sometimes, the hard problem is unrelated to the software, which is someone else's problem.

Most systems are part of a competitive landscape. We must, therefore, ask this question: What is our competitive advantage? If the competitive advantage is in the software, we have to work hard to achieve that. By definition, good competitive advantages are difficult. Otherwise, your competition would have already accomplished that or will do it once they figure it out. We can't achieve sustainable competitive advantages by doing as little as possible.

If your hard problems do not give you competitive advantages, then there is a good chance you can learn about hard problems from others. Likely, others have done it before, which can save you a lot of time and money. If a hard problem provides a competitive advantage, you must invest your time and energy in solving it. You need to invest in those as PoCs, independently of the system's design.

You need to start this process as early as possible. To do so, we should first ask the question: What is the minimal implementation that tests the idea? Then we should conduct a PoC to test it. We should bring the PoCs into the system after eliminating uncertainties in the simplest way possible.

In summary, we need to identify hard problems and handle them differently. Postponing them is not advantageous. We should identify problems that need long-term work and start fixing them early on, giving us time to get them right.

Seven Principles: The Overarching Concepts

Several overarching concepts (tactics) will help us achieve good software architecture. However, they may not always help, so we must evaluate them against the end goal of the system and use what is helpful.

Principle 1: Drive Everything from the User's Journey

The user journey defines what they can and will do with the system. It is not what is written down in the requirement specification. It is everything that can happen. The user journey, however, is never fully defined. It evolves as the user evolves and includes almost unlimited possibilities. For example, if we consider a bookstore, the user journey is what people do when they come in, and that is never fully defined. Do users want to search by the number of pages in the book? Do they want a specific author, or are they looking for a specific topic? Perhaps the user journey in this instance is to look only at journals.

We must strive to understand the user journey in as much detail as possible, covering the most important scenarios. Doing so provides a basis for building great UX and stops us from building unnecessary features.

UX makes or breaks a system. To provide a vivid example, "The Secret Startup That Saved the Worst Website in America," by Robinson Meyer explains how bad user experiences at Healthcare.gov almost broke the Affordable Care Act (ACA).[2] Many users gave up when registering, even though the alternative was not being able to go to a hospital when needed—the UX stopped even desperate users! UX alone does not make our systems successful, but without a good UX, our users won't have a chance.

The greatest source of errors in our architectures is unused or rarely used features, wasting time and money spent on them. The first step in reducing such features is to understand the user journey and evaluate everything in terms of the feature's utility to the user and the cost of forgoing the feature. We should build things that add value, not things that are easy regardless of the value.

Most systems have multiple groups of users who are interested in different parts of the user journey. We can never support all the users in all aspects of the user journey. We must choose one or the other. We have to make those choices deliberately and continuously. We return to

---

2. https://www.theatlantic.com/technology/archive/2015/07/the-secret-startup-saved-healthcare-gov-the-worst-website-in-america/397784/

this topic in the second principle. Furthermore, when we make a decision about the architecture, we need to consider these additional questions:

- How does this affect the user journey?

- How much value does it add?

- Is there something else we can do that adds more value?

Principle 2: Use an Iterative Thin Slice Strategy

Premature optimization is the root of all evil. —Donald Knuth

There are two ways to build systems. The first approach is to build all the parts and then integrate them. In my experience, most problems surface in the integration step, often adding months, if not years, to the project. The second approach creates a thin slice of the system that goes end to end and is useful at each step, using the most simple architectural choices. Then we identify bottlenecks and improve those, add new features, and replace anything only later, implementing complex architectural choices as needed.

When we are writing a basic application, this means getting the main path working as soon as possible, not worrying about the performance in the first round, then profiling the system and improving it to handle bottlenecks. With advanced compilers like JIT (Just In Time) that do many optimizations, it is tough to guess what parts need special handling. It is better to write simple code and optimize it only if and when needed.

Using this approach with a distributed app is a bit harder; however, the same idea works. Start with the most straightforward architecture and iteratively improve it. This also means integrating and merging new code as soon as possible. In other words, do small commits.

The Wright brothers are a great example of the power of this approach. Working with limited funds to build an airplane, they competed against well-funded professionals. Their competitors focused on creating the best design, building the plane, and then flying it. Opponents thought (perhaps, arrogantly) that they could think through all contingencies and build a plane that would fly on the first run. However, every time it failed to fly, it *wrecked* the prototype, setting them back months.

In contrast, the Wright brothers used an iterative *thin slice* strategy. They focused on first building a glider that worked, one that could land successfully, and then preserving the prototype. This strategy enabled them to do many more test flights. They perfected the glider and figured out how to control it. Then they added propellers and engines, gradually converting the glider into an airplane. This approach allowed them to learn, to tinker, and to experiment without months of setbacks at each failure.

An iterative thin slice strategy creates a powerful feedback cycle. This thin slice approach enabled the Wright brothers to improve gradually while in competition with much greater brain power and millions of dollars.

Unless you have a specific reason, always start with simple architectural choices. Measure the system, find the bottlenecks, and improve the system later; choose complex architectures only if needed. (Parts II and III describe some default choices and more complex selections for many situations.)

When undertaking the thin slice strategy, I have seen that simple architectures are enough to support systems over the years. A great example comes from threading models where the request per thread (with a pool) is inefficient, and nonblocking architectures can do much better. However, the resulting code from nonblocking models is harder to read, and it is not easy to find people experienced in writing this code. For many use cases, a simple request per thread model is sufficient throughout its life cycle. Let's keep our systems as simple as possible, starting unambiguously and then gradually adding complexity.

Another advantage of the thin slice strategy is that it forces everyone to integrate code early, fixing any misunderstandings about design before they come to a head and become overwhelming. This strategy works because it rapidly creates a working system, unlocking feedback, and enables us to uncover integration problems early. This approach gives us the time and the opportunity to improve and fix any problem we might encounter.

Principle 3: On Each Iteration, Add the Most Value for the Least Effort to Support More Users

As discussed, when designing the software architecture, we want to use an iterative approach that starts with limited features and then gets user feedback to improve the system. On each iteration, we want to add the most value for the least amount of effort. This means avoiding features that have little value, delaying less value-adding features to later iterations. It is important to note that most systems have many different user groups, and certain features add unique value for different users.

The user journey provides a powerful lens for making feature-related decisions. In most products, many users do only a few critical things. Find those and optimize for them. Doing this is the secret behind Apple's legendary UX. The podcast "Inside the Apple Factory: Software Design in the Age of Steve Jobs" describes Apple's approach in detail.[3] At Apple, about one-third of most teams are UX experts, so their UX quality is not an accident; they invest in it. Also, at Apple, any feature starts with the product lead (or product manager) and UX experts who then do mockups and iterations for stakeholders until the design is perfect. The code comes later.

Investing in such a process early on removes a lot of future changes and also provides a strong basis for accepting or rejecting future feature requests. Consequently, features won't be what is easy to implement but what is required by the end user.

---

3. https://www.youtube.com/watch?v=kI2Flp4oK-g

The first step for this principle is defining value. This step can mean supporting the most number of users, users who bring the most revenue, or users who can give the product the most exposure. We may even use different value criteria at different stages of the product. Examine the user journey to identify features that would add the most value by focusing on user groups that bring in the most value. In line with this principle, the following are concepts I try to follow:

- Principle 3.1: It is impossible to thoroughly think through how users will use your product, so embrace a minimum viable product (MVP). The idea is to identify a few use cases, do only features that support those cases, get feedback, and shape the product based on the feedback and experience from the MVP.

- Principle 3.2: Do as few features as possible. When in doubt (e.g., when the team disagrees), leave it out. Many features are never used, so you might develop an extension point instead.

- Principle 3.3: Wait for someone to ask for the feature. If the feature is not a deal-breaker, wait until three people ask for it before focusing on implementation.

- Principle 3.4: Have the courage to stand your ground if the features the customer requests adversely affect the product. Focus on the bigger picture and try to find another way to handle the problem.

   Remember the quote often attributed to Henry Ford: "If I had asked people what they wanted, they would have said faster horses." Also remember that *you are the expert*. You are supposed to lead. It is the leader's job to do what is right, not what is popular. Users will thank you later (fourth principle).

- Principle 3.5: Look out for Google envy. Do not overengineer. We all like shiny designs. It is easy to bring features and solutions into your architecture that you will never need. For features such as quality of service (QOS) improvements, scale, and performance limitations, wait until those requirements are imminent. Also, approach the product with the mindset that you will rewrite it. Implement what you want now.[4]

- Principle 3.6: When possible, use middleware tools or cloud services. For example, consider authentication and authorization. If you decide to implement these, it will create a lot of feature requirements in the future. For instance, you will need a user registration flow, password recovery, and attack detection. Using an identity and access management (IAM) tool supports all those features, and IAM will continue to evolve its product as requirements change. The same idea applies to message brokers, workflow systems, payment systems, and so forth.

- Principle 3.7: Interfaces and other abstractions are techniques for creating options and delaying decisions. Use them carefully. Like financial options, software options also

---

4. For details, see "You Are Not Google" at https://blog.bradfieldcs.com/you-are-not-google-84912cf44afb.

have costs. Learn to be mindful of them. Know that this presents a trade-off, thus a judgment call and, hence, a leader's responsibility. For example, a common mistake, or anti-pattern, is too many abstraction layers, which creates a terrible performance impact when we ignore the cost of abstractions.

This UX approach should go beyond UIs. We must use the same approach with APIs and internal and external messages because these formats are hard to change later. Create those APIs and message formats, iterate, and get feedback. Remember, we must design deeply but implement as little as possible.

There is one exception to implementing features as late as possible. This minimal approach does not work with features you'll need as a competitive advantage or for security. You must invest in them independently of the design process. The sixth principle addresses these unknowns.

Principle 4: Make Decisions and Absorb the Risks

The most senior technical person in the project (whom I call the chief architect) must make decisions and absorb the risks. Any project faces many uncertainties; for example, how much load and latency limits should the first version of the system have? The reality is that, often, nobody knows that number. We often ask customers, and they do not know it either. However, someone has to put down the numbers so that the team can go ahead and hit the target date. Without a target, the team can lose much time in indecision.

Richard Rumelt's book *Good Strategy, Bad Strategy* (Profile Books, 2011) provides a great example of this principle. When beginning to design a moon rover, nobody knew the moon's surface. The team designing the first such vehicle was stuck. Phyllis Buwalda, director of NASA's Future Mission Space Studies team, wrote a specification for the moon's surface based on the toughest desert on Earth. She understood that unless she took the risk of specifying the target, much time would go to waste. By writing the specification, she absorbed the uncertainty on her shoulders, thus enabling the team to make real progress.

Similarly, the chief architect must collect the required data, perform the necessary experiments, and yet, at the end, understand the unresolvable uncertainties (such as how much load the system will get) and make decisions that set concrete targets. Leaders must remove ambiguity and create targets that are solvable.

Principle 5: Design Deeply Things That Are Hard to Change but Implement Them Slowly

In my opinion, this fifth principle is the crux of designing software systems. We should design deeply but implement slowly. Let's explore what this means.

I usually advocate simple designs and adding complexity only when needed. However, some parts of the design are hard to change, such as

- APIs exposed directly to customers

- APIs of highly shared services

- Database schemas (if we deploy a product that uses a database in the customer premises)

- Shared data, objects, and message formats

- Technology frameworks

When designing, we need to expend significant energy in designing parts like APIs and database schemas. These designs must go through a lot of reviews and iterations before putting them out to the customer. For example, with APIs, even if we version those that are exposed to our customers, old releases hang around for a long time. They are hard to change, even beyond a rewrite. APIs of shared services are also difficult to change because that would require coordinated releases.

To understand what is hard to change, we must design the system deeply. At the design level, we need to dive thoroughly into creating a design that can potentially solve the entire problem and even create PoCs as needed. Having a potential design opens our eyes to possible surprises and enables us to learn more from evidence as they come up. Designing early and deeply lets us start discussions and build consensus from the start, which often consumes a lot of time.

When designing deeply, know that it's impossible to go deep into every aspect of the software due to limited time and resources. For any part of the system that we can change and evolve without affecting the rest of the system and for those that do not contain significant unknowns, we can defer the details to a later date. Doing this properly requires judgment. Unless we do this, however, we will drown in the details.

For example, writing a service is a well-understood problem, but unless we see the need for that service to handle complexity (e.g., large throughput, large messages), we can defer the implementation details after defining the APIs. In general, if an API or interface hides the implementation details and that is understood, we can delay the implementation design. Thus, designing deeply should focus on APIs, interfaces, and their interactions. We must, however, realize that the current design will be based on our incomplete understanding of the problem and will evolve over time.

The deep design does not imply an urgency to implement it. Doing things slowly lets us implement things with more understanding and helps avoid future changes. Bring about things only when your user journey analysis indicates that they are necessary and that they add significant value. Designing deeply, implementing slowly, and using the judgment required to do this efficiently and decisively are hallmarks of a great architect.

Principle 6: Eliminate the Unknowns and Learn from the Evidence by Working on Hard Problems Early and in Parallel

Detect unknowns early and systematically eliminate them rather than trusting your luck. Often this effort requires experiments to resolve them, which is one of the chief architect's key responsibilities. Resolving unknowns requires trial and error, which usually takes time. Proactively exploring unknowns gives us enough time to inspect those problems and find the right solutions. This foresight differentiates a great architect from a good one.

Kelly Johnson, the aircraft designer, offers a great example. Designing aircraft for Defense Advanced Research Projects Agency (DARPA), his team built the first aircraft that goes three times faster than sound (Mach 3). Wind tunnels at that time could not simulate wing design at this speed. Kelly found a simple solution: He collected data by borrowing 400 missiles, mounted different wing designs on them, and conducted experiments.

Experiments are a crucial tool in any designer's arsenal. Because it is much easier to do experiments with software than with an aircraft; we have little excuse for not doing them. One of my advisors used to say never argue or analyze something that you can check with fifteen minutes of code.

This principle also ties in with the deep design that allows us to proactively identify unknowns beyond what is apparent at first glance. If we believe a certain part of the design is unknown and risky, we need to dig into that part early to give us time to resolve the unknown.

There is a second related point. With software, it is easy to rerun something. Yet, we do not want to build monitoring into the system and are bad at collecting enough data to understand what is really happening. Ironically, because it is easy to collect the data, we never collect it. Yet, complex problems and situations do not happen often and are hard to recreate. Unless we collect data, it is hard to learn from these situations, robbing us of an opportunity to fix bugs and to deeply understand the system.

In contrast, designers in many other disciplines such as vehicle design, aeronautics, and medicine have only a few experiments about a particular topic at their disposal. Hence, they collect a lot of data and usually know much more about their systems than software professionals do.

We should add monitoring into our systems early and take the time to instrument it. For example, we can measure operating system telematics, queue sizes, selected traces, timed breakdowns, and throughput at different places in our system. Also, because it is not practical to comb through the data daily, we should automate the analysis process as much as possible. Careful monitoring enables us to learn a lot from every situation.

Monitoring has a minor performance penalty. Yet, in the long run, we will save money by building better systems. This kind of monitoring is essential for the feedback loop if we operate within tight performance constraints.

Principle 7: Understand the Trade-offs Between Cohesion and Flexibility in the Software Architecture

As budding architects, we learned about the principles of flexibility and cohesion in the architecture. Venkat Subramaniam's talks are a great source for understanding these principles.[5] However, most of these principles have costs too. Hence, software architecture must be evaluated in its context, which we explored in the five questions, but sometimes we have to break the principles to create the best architecture.

Flexibility refers to the ability of the system to change. As mentioned, flexibility also costs and can be more expensive. For example, as we discussed earlier in this chapter, flexibility to run on multiple clouds can, on average, be more expensive than building for one cloud and redesigning if and when it's needed.

Cohesion broadly means that architectural concepts are applied throughout the system. A common thing to check is whether the system reuses its components or services everywhere. An ideal system should be composed of services or components that handle one aspect (e.g., only logging, security, messaging, registry, mediation, or analytics), and all parts of the system must reuse those aspects when needed without reimplementing them. If you need configuration parsing, use configuration parsing components. If you need logs, use the logging component. This extends the DRY principle (Don't Repeat Yourself) from code to architecture.

In modern architectures, this reuse can happen at the library level (same process) or at the service level. Unfortunately, trying to enforce this principle too rigidly can lead to problems. For example, asking every service to call a configuration service or query builder service can be too much (but not always). Sometimes, bringing in a component can also be too complicated because it brings in other dependent components in turn. Simple features can cascade into significant changes. I saw an example of this, where adding mediation dependency to an identity server added hundreds of new dependencies.

The most unfortunate use of cohesion happens as follows: We detect some aspects of one service that can be reused by another service and ask the first team to refactor and create a new service or a component. The second team incorporates this service into their system. This kind of refactoring, which forces close communication between multiple teams, should be done only when it is absolutely necessary.

Usually, it is not worth doing this to reduce duplication slightly. I have done this and paid the price. With hindsight, I am now willing to live with some level of duplication and inconsistencies when fixing those results in significant complexity. The cure, sometimes, can be worse than the disease.

It is useful to think about architecture as a way to build systems that are cheaper in the long run and tactics as tools in your toolbox. We use tools only when they make sense. In the next section, we look at a sample system to explore how to use these questions and principles.

---

5. See http://alex-ii.github.io/notes/2017/12/09/core_design_principles.html.

Designing for an Online Bookstore

As a running example, let's consider an online bookshop, where users can search for rare books, order them, make payments, and then track the order until it is delivered. It also includes returns and any after-sales services. This example will show us how to use the concepts mentioned in this chapter in real use cases.

As previously noted, a solid design process begins with an understanding of the business context. Take, for example, a bookstore, which can range from being quite simple (like a friendly neighborhood bookstore that announces new arrivals via WhatsApp) to extremely complex (like Amazon). These differences are shaped by the unique business context.

It falls to leadership to ensure the business context isn't lost when faced with making tough choices or trade-offs at the information system or technology levels. We've already discussed five questions that aid in understanding the business and technical context, as well as seven principles for iteratively improving the system's design in the realm of software architecture.

Furthermore, as we've previously discussed, our conversation primarily centers on the design layer of the information system.

First, let's consider the business context. We have six months to take the product to market with an average team. Our initial goal is to establish the product in the market. We do not know how much load we can expect. However, the back-of-a-napkin calculator shows us 50–100 TPS (Transactions per Second) throughput, which means that the business will be in good shape. It is fair to assume that we can rewrite the system at that point.

A developer cannot make this decision; one of the leaders has to make it, which is an example of the fourth principle. The two unknowns are transaction processing at scale and book recommendations. We are able to differentiate the first problem because we need only 50–100 TPS. We need to start exploring the recommendations soon because this is unknown to the team.

As per the first principle, we should start by understanding the user journey. My recommendation is to start with a UX design. In my experience, writing a requirement specification does not work well because neither designers, developers, nor users can see the fine points in the design without experiencing the system. We need an iterative approach. A mocked UX lets everyone experience the system and iterate it.

As we alluded to previously, the design has many levels of recursive abstractions. A typical system would have a macro-level architecture that describes different services, data stores, and other middleware and how they relate to each other. Then, each service would have an architecture that describes different components and how they relate to each other, and each component would have an architecture on the code level and how those code segments relate to each other. This book focuses primarily on the first two levels. We discuss how to architect the overall system in Chapters 5–10 and how to architect individual services in Chapter 11.

Having narrowed down the UX, we should focus on the macro architecture. Figure 2.1 shows a typical macro architecture for the bookstore. Typical software architecture in the 2020s would use databases to store the state: a set of (stateless) services that handle business logic. Those services are used in one of three ways: a single-page application (SPA) running in the browser, a mobile app, or direct API calls. (Chapters 5–10 discuss these in more detail.)

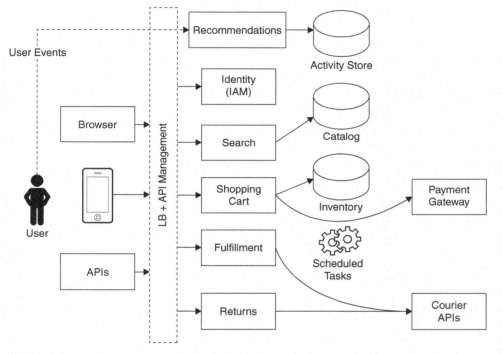

Figure 2.1
A typical macro architecture for the online bookstore.

Services are loosely coupled with other services. If we use microservices concepts in our macro architecture, each service can be developed, released, and deployed independently. Identifying services given a problem is called *service decomposition*, which is a crucial skill of an architect. Chapter 5 discusses it in more detail under SOA.

Once we have identified services, the next step is to identify interservice interactions and to define message formats (APIs) for those interactions. At this point, our "do as little as possible" approach applies some friction.

It is hard to change the message formats or API of a widely used service later. We must spend time thinking through these interactions and develop a mature set of APIs. We can use user interactions identified in our UX design in this phase. Following the fifth principle, at this point, we should design deeply, define message formats, and think through immediate and long-term use cases. As part of thinking deeply, we should also define the database schema.

When we deeply design both schemas and APIs, it clarifies most of the design. It is a good idea to take a lot of feedback and discussion about APIs and databases to ensure we get them right.

As mentioned, we implement slowly, learning and revising the design as we go on. A far-reaching API design gives us a broad and balanced understanding of the system. Public APIs need extra care, however. If well-defined message standards exist, we should adopt them as much as possible. For example, using JWT (JSON Web Tokens) tokens for authentication saves us the need to define a token format and also gives us the flexibility to change our identity server later.

Once we have a design, we should plan the implementation. As principles 2 and 3 mention, we should first identify a thin slice and get that working. This could be the ability to see a book, select it, and order it. Each iteration after that should create features to maximize the value they add. For example, iterations can add search, shopping cart, returns, recommendations, and so on to our online bookstore.

In parallel, as per principle 6, we need to start exploring hard problems such as recommendations and even scalable transaction processing. The reason is that we need time to get them right.

After identifying the abstract architecture, while implementing iterations, we should design our services. We can do this by deciding which parts to develop, which parts to reuse, and how to implement them. Here are some examples:

- We can implement each service using tools like Spring Boot and MySQL. For services such as IAM and payment APIs, we can use either an off-the-shelf middleware or an SaaS (Software as a Service) solution.

- We can implement fulfillment and return services using a message queue or a workflow system, due to their asynchronous and long-running nature.

The final choice needs to factor in considerations such as time to market, required performance, and the experience of the team. My recommendation is to start simple and add complexity as needed unless you have prior experience in building similar systems.

At some point in the middle of development, we should take the product to customers. This point is called *minimum viable product* or *minimum lovable product*. It can start with friendly users and expand to more and more users.

At each step, we should strive to learn. Although we have a design, we can modify it if our learning suggests changes. Note that this process continues as long as the system is live.

From the viewpoint of TOGAF's three layers, the majority of the architecture we've talked about falls into the category of information systems architecture. Yet, most decisions are influenced by the business context, which expands upon TOGAF's business architecture. We delve into technology architecture only when we discuss specific technologies, like Spring Boot or MySQL, and that's mainly done as examples or to illustrate complexity.

Designing for the Cloud

Several exciting possibilities open up if we are designing the system for the cloud. We have two choices:

- Shallow cloud integration: We write our services, pack them as containers, and run them in the cloud using cloud services for databases and storage only. Such a design architecturally behaves similarly to on-premises systems.

- Deep cloud integration: We build the system using the cloud as much as possible, replacing all services with serverless functions and as much functionality with cloud and SaaS services.

Figure 2.2 shows an example of architecture for a bookshop that uses the cloud as much as possible.

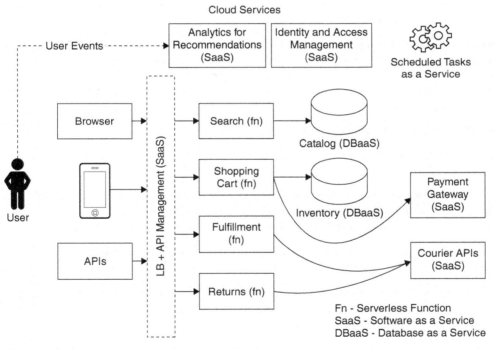

Figure 2.2
Software architecture for a bookshop that uses the cloud.

Choosing such an architecture yields several advantages. First, it provides a faster time to market because it

- Needs less coding and configuration

- Avoids boilerplate code such as security logic with configurations

- Replaces functionality with API calls

- Focuses on business logic instead of plumbing

- Provides HA, scalability, and DevOps out of the box

Second, it lowers platform costs by providing a true, pay-as-you-go model while eliminating idle time costs. Most applications have variable loads. However, according to the central limit theorem, when many of those variable loads are aggregated, the resulting workload has a predictable distribution curve even if the individual workloads are not predictable. Consequently, cloud platforms can operate with fewer resources despite the additional overhead. As a result, cloud providers enjoy substantial savings through economies of scale, which they can pass on to the users.

Third, cloud platforms lower development costs by taking over DevOps and monitoring costs. Cloud platforms can deliver DevOps and monitoring for a fraction of the cost, using economies of scale, tools, and optimized operations. They can also pass on some of those savings to the end user, creating a win-win situation for both.

Fourth, cloud architectures provide predictable costs, tying costs to the amount of work the system receives, thus reducing capital expenditures and the risks of operating the system. Usually, doing more work brings organizations more money; hence, having cost tied to future revenues is a welcome development. Because cloud platforms are metered with fine granularity, they provide greater insights into managing costs.

Cloud-based architectures also have disadvantages:

- A deep cloud integration invariably creates a lock-in restriction, making it hard and expensive to move away from a cloud provider after going to production.

- Using the cloud requires the team to learn new programming models. Furthermore, cloud platforms are opinionated, forcing programmers to follow preset patterns, allowing users little or no leverage to get those fixed if cloud features do not fit well with their requirements.

- The cloud can be more expensive than other options if the system receives a significant load around the clock.

An architect must balance these pros and cons and decide on which approach to use, based on the key questions we discussed in this chapter. Sometimes, it may be more economical to accept the lock-in and commit to rewriting if we have to move out of the cloud.

Next, we move on to Part II, where we discuss performance and UX concepts, which are key tools for good design. However, if you do not want to delve into technical details, you can skip to Part III, where we discuss macro-level and micro-level design.

Summary

Following are key takeaways from this chapter:

- Software architecture is a plan to build a software system.

- The overarching goal of creating a software system (hence, for software architecture) is to meet quality standards and ones that are more economical in the long run.

- Although there are essential tactics (e.g., making code easy to change, avoiding lock-in), we should evaluate each of those tactics not as something that stands alone but as something that is a part of the whole. For example, sometimes, it might make sense to accept lock-in and go to the cloud if in the long run it is cheaper to rewrite the system than switching to a new cloud provider.

- The best design depends on the context. Hence, it is a matter of judgment.

- We discussed five questions and seven principles that can help us make the right judgment calls when designing and implementing software systems. We saw those questions and principles in action by way of an example.

3

Mental Models for Understanding and Explaining System Performance

Performance is an inseparable factor in software architecture. It dictates the limits of possibilities when creating the system. On the one hand, we try to design systems that are easy to understand, learn, and change. On the other hand, we have to meet performance targets, which forces us to use more complex and exotic techniques, increasing the complexity of the design. Architects must learn to master the balance between the two.

It is useful to define *business performance* as the average output per unit cost incurred over time. For example, if you represent a company, the business performance can be described as the amount of money you make per unit of money spent on a computer system, including the cost of programmers, project management, and software licenses. This definition lets us approach performance holistically.

Architects should design to maximize business performance in the long run. This is why we do not code everything in assembly. For software architectures, we should consider the time to market, the skill levels of the team, and our potential returns and user expectations.

It is much easier to be a great architect if you have an intuitive feel for the system's performance. This chapter aims to give you that understanding. To have an intuitive feel for the performance, we need to have some mental models (simply a representation of how something works) about the computer while it is working.

One common belief about computer performance is that the CPU limits its capabilities. If this is true, then if we write each part of the program as optimally as possible, it should run optimally. To do so, we can find where the most time is spent using a CPU profiler and improve the code to minimize this limitation.

You have likely encountered a program that refuses to run any faster, although the host computer does not use much CPU or memory while running the program. You have tuned, profiled, and even begged to no avail. This phenomenon gives us an insight into the limits of performance on a computer.

If our applications can keep up with the expected load, all is well; otherwise, we tune the system. We start with a CPU profile, inspect database calls (e.g., review the slow query log) and memory, and tune thread pools, among other checks.

The 80/20 rule for programs facilitates tuning. This rule states that in a system a few code segments run most of the time. Hence, we can improve performance by finding and fixing hot spots and resource hogs. These improvements can make systems go significantly faster, even as much as several times faster. We tune iteratively, finding bottlenecks and fixing them until we reach the point where significant improvements are no longer possible.

Sometimes the system lags behind the expected limits even after tuning while the machine is lightly loaded (e.g., 60% CPU usage). Understanding why this is so is the key to understanding computer performance.

This chapter describes eight mental models that help us think about and understand performance, which facilitates our knowledge of why the system is not using any leftover CPU. Furthermore, we see that most performance limitations stem from the architecture, and these models can also be used to make architecture choices at design time.

The next section provides some background about computer systems. In the section following that one, we introduce six models, which we call six micro models. Two additional models to optimize for throughput and performance are also introduced in this chapter. The following chapters present more detail about these last two models. The remaining sections in this chapter discuss specific optimization techniques.

This chapter is more detailed and technical compared to the other chapters. These specifics are crucial, and they aren't widely covered in other books. If you're initially seeking a broader understanding, you could briefly go through this chapter, but I recommend revisiting it to grasp the finer points eventually.

A Computer System

A computer consists of many kinds of resources, which we use to run applications, and applications help us attain some goals. The operating system (OS) manages the first three resources here:

- **CPU:** Our code uses the CPU through OS processes (or threads) that support time-sharing. Current computers have many CPUs, and it is possible to pin a process to a CPU, thus giving it exclusive access.

- **Memory:** Our code allocates memory and uses it, although some program languages take over memory management by supporting garbage collection (GC). This usage, however, adds a GC overhead. A cache hierarchy fronts memory and reduces memory access latency.

- **Network and disk:** Our code accesses network and disk resources via the OS's I/O interfaces. Both resources have the same limitations: input/output operations per second (IOPS) and bandwidth.

- **Other resources (often called *soft resources*):** Among examples are database connection pools, object pools, locks, and queues.

Our code uses the first three resources exclusively. The OS lets us share resources either by time-sharing or partitioning the resource.

I use the term *application* (or *app*) to describe a program running in a computer system. An application is a collection of tasks using a subset of resources.

In the following discussion, we focus on the server's performance because most software architectures are exclusively built on servers. However, we can use the same techniques and concepts with other systems such as desktop applications, daemons, and batch tasks.

Models for Performance

This chapter introduces several models for thinking about performance. Mental models are simple representations of how something works, and you can find examples of mental models at https://fs.blog/mental-models/. This book introduces additional new mental models targeting system performance.

Let's start with the main idea, explain it via an analogy, and then discuss the models in detail.

Consider a hotel buffet that has soups, the main course, and desserts. Let's assume that the output is the number of people served per hour. We observe that when the output is highest, some parts (e.g., dessert first and soup later) may be idling. Bottlenecks cause this observation, where the most constrained resource decides performance. For example, the article "Big List of Common Bottlenecks" provides a list of common bottlenecks that we see in systems.[1]

If we want to maximize the number of meals served, we can get the best performance by using the "computer" as fully and effectively as possible, which we do by removing bottlenecks. This is the key idea behind Brendan Gregg's talk, "CPU Utilization Is Wrong," at the 16th annual Southern California Linux Expo.[2] The seventh model describes this for maximum throughput.

---

1. http://highscalability.com/blog/2012/5/16/big-list-of-20-common-bottlenecks.html

2. https://opensource.com/article/18/4/cpu-utilization-wrong

Often, latency (the time it takes to serve a meal in the restaurant, for example) also matters. If I have to wait three hours to get my meal, it's unlikely I will return. Our software also needs to operate within latency limits. The eighth model explains this scenario.

The models, described next, give us insight into how computers work. The first six models are behavioral micro models of performance.

Model 1: Cost of Switching to the Kernel Mode from the User Mode

A computer OS has two modes: user and kernel. The code we write runs in user mode, but the privileged operations such as performing input/output, accessing memory, and changing kernel data structures run in kernel mode. Every time an application enters kernel mode, a context switch occurs, which adds nonessential costs to the system, such as time to save the stack and to rest the cache. To improve performance, we need to reduce the number of system calls.

Model 2: Operations Hierarchy

A computer execution performs a wide range of operations, ranging from cache access, memory access, and disk and network operations. Figure 3.1 shows the costs of those operations (based on Jeff Dean's talk, "Designs, Lessons and Advice from Building Large Distributed Systems").[3] This list is a bit older, but it is still good enough to make a point. Let's call this our *operations hierarchy*.

```
Latency Comparison Numbers (~2012)
----------------------------------
L1 cache reference                      0.5 ns
Branch mispredict                       5   ns
L2 cache reference                      7   ns                    14x L1 cache
Mutex lock/unlock                       25  ns
Main memory reference                   100 ns                    20x L2 cache, 200x L1 cache
Compress 1K bytes with Zippy          3,000 ns        3 us
Send 1K bytes over 1 Gbps network    10,000 ns       10 us
Read 4K randomly from SSD*          150,000 ns      150 us        ~1GB/sec SSD
Read 1 MB sequentially from memory  250,000 ns      250 us
Round trip within same datacenter   500,000 ns      500 us
Read 1 MB sequentially from SSD*  1,000,000 ns    1,000 us   1 ms  ~1GB/sec SSD, 4X memory
Disk seek                        10,000,000 ns   10,000 us  10 ms  20x datacenter roundtrip
Read 1 MB sequentially from disk 20,000,000 ns   20,000 us  20 ms  80x memory, 20X SSD
Send packet CA->Netherlands->CA 150,000,000 ns  150,000 us 150 ms
```

Figure 3.1
Operations hierarchy and associated costs.

---

3. http://www.cs.cornell.edu/projects/ladis2009/talks/dean-keynote-ladis2009.pdf

As Figure 3.1 depicts, faster operations proceed at thousands to a million times faster than slower operations. This means that sometimes we are justified in doing more work to avoid slower operations. For example, if we can stop a single I/O operation, we can afford to do 5,000 memory operations in its place.

Model 3: Context Switching Overhead

To create an illusion of multitasking, the OS preempts current processes once it has run for a while. This leads to a *context switch*, which creates three adverse outcomes:

- Switching processes adds an overhead cost of about 5–7 microseconds.[4]

- When a process comes back, it loses data in the cache.

- The time to finish the task increases due to interleaving with other processes.

As the number of threads increases, these overhead costs increase.[5] Therefore, if you have thousands of threads, the system wastes a significant amount of time doing context switching. We call this *thrashing* when the cost becomes excessive.

Model 4: Amdahl's Law

Amdahl's law describes the limit imposed on concurrent processing due to synchronization.[6] We use multiple threads or processes in a system to get things done faster (e.g., achieve a speedup). We define speedup as follows:

$$\text{Speedup} = \frac{\text{Time to finish the program with } N \text{ threads or processes}}{\text{Time to finish the program with one thread or process}}$$

Figure 3.2 depicts Amdhal's law. It provides an upper bound for speedup when we perform a task using *n* parallel executions.

---

4. https://stackoverflow.com/questions/21887797/what-is-the-overhead-of-a-context-switch

5. https://en.wikipedia.org/wiki/Completely_Fair_Scheduler

6. https://en.wikipedia.org/wiki/Amdahl%27s_law

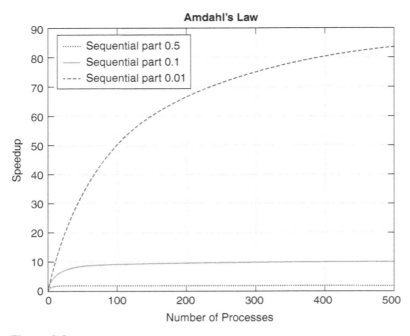

Figure 3.2
Speedup and Amdahl's law.

For example, if you have an exclusive lock covering all the programs, only one thread runs, irrespective of the other code. If you have a lock covering 50% of the program, then the maximum speedup possible is twice as fast, regardless of the number of threads in the system. Amdahl's law suggests that the best solution is *not* to use blocking synchronization at all.

Model 5: Universal Scalability Law (USL)

Universal Scalability Law says that actual speedup is even worse than Amdahl's law due to shared variables. USL defines a new parameter coherency, which is the overhead added by communication between multiple processes, threads, or nodes.

Figure 3.3 shows both Amdahl's law and USL. Here, the line on the top shows speedup with a 0.01 sequential part, and the USL line shows speedup with a 0.01 sequential part and 0.001 coherency. You can see that the speedup allowed by USL is even smaller and more drastically limiting (50 times speedup with 100 processes or 80 times speedup with 400 processes). This means that we should also minimize shared variables among processes, threads, or nodes that force interprocess communication.

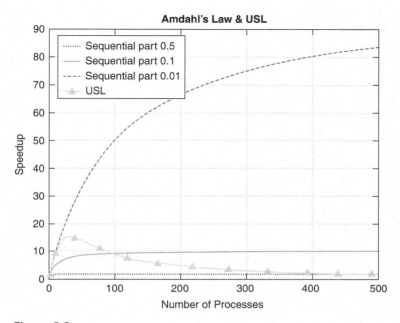

Figure 3.3
Speedup and the Universal Scalability Law (USL) compared to Amdahl's.

Model 6: Latency and Utilization Trade-offs

Only a single thread can use the most resources at a given time, which forces threads to wait and take turns. As the utilization of the system increases, the processes have to wait longer on average for resources to become available. This wait increases the latency that users experience. Because most applications must respond within latency bounds, they can't afford to utilize the system entirely. We can explain this model formally using queueing theory.[7]

Model 7: Designing for Throughput with the Maximal Useful Utilization (MUU) Model

A given system attains maximum throughput when we meet the following conditions:

- Each sequential task is implemented optimally (we can fix this via profiling).

- Nonessential tasks are minimal (e.g., GC, context switching, communication overhead, and cache misses).

- Use the most limiting resource maximally

---

7. https://en.wikipedia.org/wiki/Queueing_theory

Tasks are assigned to threads and other resources such that the resource in most demand is used to do the most important work. Typically, we do this by keeping the utilization of the most restrictive resource highest, the next restrictive resource next highest, and so on.

The first two conditions are self-explanatory. However, the third one needs some explanation. The third condition describes how to allocate resources optimally. It says idling computing resources is a waste, just like a grounded plane is a waste in the eyes of airline companies. If a computer resource is assigned to a thread or process exclusively but not used, it is wasted. For example, if we assign employees in our restaurant to specific tables when some tables are not in use, the associated employees idle.

Exclusive resources force threads to wait for each other and take turns. Correct order and timing significantly affect the performance of systems. For example, the CPU is often the most critical resource because all programs use the CPU. If we assign programs directly to the CPU, a blocked thread or a processor can choke and idle the CPU. Hence, the OS undergoes time-sharing to reduce the probability. Even then, the system wastes the CPU when there is no active process for every CPU core. For instance, if you have an eight-thread program running on an eight-core machine while blocking I/O operations, most cores will idle because most threads are waiting for I/O most of the time.

Such waste happens when many processes are blocked or waiting. We can add more threads, hoping that at least a few of them will be ready at a given time. However, adding more threads increases the context switch overhead (nonessential work) and resets most caches. Now we have a trade-off of waste due to idleness versus context switches. One corollary of this model is that when the CPU is the limiting resource, we should reduce blocking and the number of threads as much as possible.

The CPU is not always the most restrictive resource, however. For example, the CPU may have to wait until data arrives in the system, in which case, the disk may be the most restrictive resource. In such cases, we need to optimize for the disk by caching or prefetching data (in effect, giving up memory and CPU to optimize disk reads).

A program has many data, control, and resource dependencies. Hence, it is often not possible to use all the resources. We get the best performance by maximizing the utilization of the most restrictive resource. The thread model decides where and when a given resource is used and, consequently, its utilization. Because the thread model is hard to change without a rewrite, we should address this issue at design time.

Note that the following performance model is defined only for throughput. For servers, we need to consider latency as well, which we discuss later (in model 8).

This MUU model applies to single-node applications as well as to distributed applications. In the latter case, we count communication overheads as nonessential tasks. We can explain most performance advice and best practices using the three conditions previously mentioned.

Coming back to MUU, due to the bottlenecks and sixth model (latency and utilization trade-offs), an application running in four to eight or more cores is rarely able to attain full utilization for those cores. Hence, the best we can do is to use the most limiting resource maximally.

In Chapter 7, we apply these mental models to different types of use cases to understand their performance behaviors and to discuss how to improve performance. It is worth noting, however, that most performance limitations stem from the architecture, and most of the techniques need significant code changes. In the next section, we discuss adding latency limits to the MUU. After that, we explore how to use the models to optimize performance.

Model 8: Adding Latency Limits

In the previous section, we focused on maximizing throughput, which we can attain by maximizing useful resource optimization as per the MUU model. Yet latency is also a key consideration for applications where users wait for results. Furthermore, in some applications, such as stock-trading and real-time applications, the primary goal is low latency rather than high throughput.

According to the sixth micro model, latency and utilization are a trade-off. As Figure 3.4 shows, when utilization goes up, latency increases exponentially. This increase happens because when we utilize a computer fully, there have to be work tasks ready for each worker thread, which means work tasks need to wait for the worker threads, which leads to higher latency.

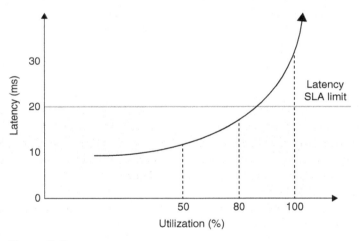

Figure 3.4
Relationship of utilization to latency.

As mentioned, higher throughput needs higher utilization. Therefore, we can say that high throughput and low latencies are a trade-off.

Most real-world applications seek to get maximum throughput within a given latency limit. For example, a server specification might say requests should be processed within 100ms, and a server implementation seeks to get maximum throughput within those limits.

Latency, however, follows a long-tail distribution, so it is tough to keep all latencies strictly below a given limit. In practice, we define the latency in terms of a percentile (e.g., requirements may ask for the 99th percentile to be kept less than 100ms).

To control latencies, we can pick an operational point within given latency limits. For example, look at the arrival rate versus latency graph in Figure 3.5.

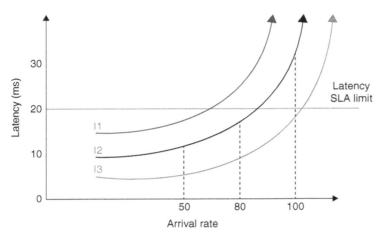

Figure 3.5
Relationship of latency vs. arrival rate.

In Figure 3.5, the items I1, I2, and I3 correspond to different implementations of the given system. A given implementation can provide different latency-throughput combinations for different arrival rates. As Figure 3.5 illustrates, given an implementation, we therefore can pick the operational point based on required latency limits by controlling the arrival rate. (Mathematically speaking, because latency is a convex function, it is straightforward to find the optimal arrival rate by trial and error.) Because at a steady state, the arrival rate would be equivalent to throughput, this also decides throughput. If we require higher throughput, we need to either improve the implementation (e.g., I3 is better than I2) or run multiple copies of the system for scale.

We control the arrival rate by monitoring and refusing requests that exceed the arrival rate. In practice, either the system notifies users and asks them to try later, or it starts a new server and diverts the requests to the new server. This is called *admission control*, and we discuss it in Chapter 12. We do, however, revisit the topic again under latency optimization techniques later in this chapter.

We call latencies that deviate significantly from the norms *tail latencies*, which are usually all values higher than the percentiles P99 or P99.9. We can't use the approaches we discussed to improve tail latencies, which are caused by events that are different from the norm, such as GC, a burst of requests, and resource sharing with other processes. To handle tail latencies, we need to identify each and then eliminate them. Although effective, the techniques to handle tail latencies are expensive, waste resources, and add more complexity. We should therefore design systems for strong latency guarantees only when necessary.

Optimization Techniques

When we have an initial version of the system, we can use optimization techniques to get better performance. These techniques may include increasing throughput, reducing latency, or making the system work with fewer resources.

To optimize, we need to decide where the bottlenecks are. Bottlenecks usually come in one of three forms:

- One of the resources (e.g., CPU, I/O, or memory) is the bottleneck.
- Thread models are causing critical resources to be idle.
- Resources are wasted on nonessential tasks (e.g., context switches, GC).

The first step is to use the system and programming language telemetry to figure out the primary bottleneck. This step includes looking at CPU, memory, and network data in the system as well as looking at thread profiles, locking profilers, and so on in the profiler. Brendan Gregg's USE method is one approach to finding the bottleneck.[8]

The next step is to fix the bottleneck because there is little to be gained by optimizing nonbottleneck areas. We can fix the bottleneck in two primary ways:

- Trading a nonbottleneck resource for a bottleneck resource
- Knowing how the system works

Let's look at a few examples for the first approach, where a cache gives up memory and CPU to reduce I/O and latency. The process of forecasting and prefetching required data gives up the CPU to save I/O and latency. Cassandra's SSTables trade CPU and memory for I/O performance by only recording change events on disk and reconstructing the state in memory to serve read requests.[9]

The second way is to know how the system works to improve performance, where the required knowledge often comes from performance mental models. Among examples are caching or buffering (the operations hierarchy model), decomposing tasks to multiple threads or consolidating tasks to a single thread (Amdahl's law and USL models), and prefetching to avoid waits (Amdahl's law). The following sections explore common techniques to optimize CPU, I/O, memory, and latency.

---

8. https://www.brendangregg.com/usemethod.html

9. http://distributeddatastore.blogspot.com/2013/08/cassandra-sstable-storage-format.html

CPU Optimization Techniques

We can work with individual tasks, memory, and core utilization to optimize the CPU. We dive into the details of each technique next.

Optimize Individual Tasks

First, we optimize individual tasks, which we can handle by finding hot spots using a profiler and by eliminating or improving them. We can get further improvements by using better algorithms, programming languages close to the hardware (e.g., assembly language), or specialized hardware such as GPUs (Graphics Processing Units) and field-programmable gate arrays (FPGAs).

Optimize Memory

Second, we can ensure memory is not getting in the way by optimizing a cache. You can find more details about this approach in the section on memory optimization techniques later in this chapter.

Maximize CPU Utilization

Third, we want to maximize CPU core utilization while doing useful work. CPU core utilization may suffer due to blocking threads or an imbalance in task allocation to threads. In the earlier section about the MUU model, we discussed how to handle blocking tasks in detail.

We can handle task imbalance by decomposing the work into smaller tasks and distributing them among many threads. However, as discussed regarding Amdahl's law and USL (models 4 and 5), when we decompose tasks, we have to minimize the synchronization and shared variables, which limits speedup. We can favorably decompose some tasks. For example, we can't make Fibonacci series calculations run faster than the serial version.

Task decomposition is complicated and studied in detail under the field of parallel computing.[10] In some cases, we don't know the complexity of the task a priori; then utilization suffers. In those cases, we have to either delay the work assignments or readjust them while the program is running. We usually handle this issue with a shared job queue from which threads take work after finishing the current task or using *work stealing*. With work stealing, idling threads borrow work from neighboring threads.[11]

---

10. https://en.wikipedia.org/wiki/Parallel_computing

11. See Robert D. Blumofe, "Scheduling Multithreaded Computations by Work Stealing," *Journal of the ACM*, vol. 46, no. 5, https://doi.org/10.1145/324133.324234.

I/O Optimization Techniques

I/O is thousands to a million times slower than other operations, which justifies going to great lengths to avoid this type of work. The following sections describe several techniques that we can use to optimize I/O.

Avoid I/O

If at all possible, avoid I/O operations. There are several ways to do this. The easiest is to use a cache, which holds often-used data in memory and avoids I/O. However, it is hard to predict the required data early on, so we need to carefully tune the cache.

We can also use a *bloom filter*, which is a probabilistic hashmap that can remember large amounts of data using a small space.[12] When queried, if the bloom filter says a key does not exist, it is always correct. When the bloom filter says yes, it does exist, it is only correct with a high probability. By fronting data in the disk with a bloom filter, we can reduce I/O by avoiding queries for things that are not in the store. If you must use I/O, do it in an asynchronous style. This approach reduces its downside due to blocking.

Buffering

I/O happens as blocks, and the cost of reading and writing each block is about the same; for example, the Linux default buffer size is 8KB. Whether you write 1KB or 8KB, the cost is about the same. We can save a lot by buffering the writes (Java-buffered streams do this automatically). If you are implementing buffering yourself, you can use the disrupter pattern, which buffers data without waiting.[13] We look at this pattern in Chapter 11.

Send Early, Receive Late, Don't Ask but Tell

If data to be processed comes through I/O, slow I/O decelerates CPU processing. To minimize the effects of slow I/O, Message Passing Interface (MPI) programming uses the maximum "Send Early, Receive Late, Don't Ask but Tell." By proactively sending data and using the data as late as possible, we maximize the chance that the data has already arrived before it's needed, which increases the performance of the system. (We can also use the same maxim in our code.)

Prefetching

Another idea is *prefetching*, which predicts the data required for processing and starts the I/O operation early, usually in a different thread to maximize the chance that data is ready when needed.

---

12. https://highlyscalable.wordpress.com/2012/05/01/probabilistic-structures-web-analytics-data-mining/

13. https://stackoverflow.com/questions/6559308/how-does-lmaxs-disruptor-pattern-work

For example, when you start typing in the search box, Google guesses your query and prefetches results from the server to reduce latency.

Append-Only Processing

While writing and reading to the disk, appends and sequential reads are much faster than random access operations. The reason is that sequential operations avoid disk rotational delay, which is the time for the sector containing the block to rotate and align with the header, adding significant delays to disk latency. With solid-state drives (SSDs), the difference is reduced but still present.[14] We can therefore improve I/O performance if we convert all reads and writes to sequential reads and writes as much as possible.

Some use cases, such as Kafka programs, naturally support append-only processing.[15] A similar optimization is still possible for other use cases as well. For example, Cassandra remembers data via a changelog, which supports sequential reads and writes, while using an in-memory table called an SS table to calculate the most recent snapshot of the data to support random reads.

Memory Optimization Techniques

Memory-bound behavior can occur in several ways. Next, let's look at two such techniques.

Too Many Cache Misses

Frequently used variables, written or read across many threads, trigger a cache miss, forcing subsequent reads of any of the variables to load the value from memory. This is about 100 times slower than reading data from the cache. Such cache misses can be expensive, and if they become the bottleneck, we call it the *memory wall*. For example, "An Analysis of Web Servers Architectures Performances on Commodity Multicores" by Sylvain Genevès shows that the load on memory increases with the number of cores saturating at eight cores.[16]

Cache misses are handled by reducing shared variables among multiple processes and then optimizing cache behavior. For example, in his talk "Adventures with Concurrent Programming in Java: A Quest for Predictable Latency," Martin Thomson describes in detail how they optimized the cache misses using Disruptor.[17] The alternative is to do all communications between processes explicitly via message passing or a queue.

---

14. https://www.quora.com/Do-append-only-DB-log-structures-benefit-from-Flash-memory-and-SSDs

15. See "Here's What Makes Kafka So Fast" at https://medium.freecodecamp.org/what-makes-apache-kafka-so-fast-a8d4f94ab145 for a detailed discussion.

16. https://hal.inria.fr/hal-00674475/document

17. https://www.youtube.com/watch?v=rKMTsJxYK30

Not Enough Memory

If the system operates at the edge of available memory, most memory operations such as GC and allocations become expensive. We can address this issue by either adding more memory, optimizing the memory, or moving some of the data to disk.

Optimizing memory may include new algorithms and data structures, freeing up data early and optimizing allocations. State-of-the-art profilers have several views that help us with memory optimizations. Also, GC overhead can become excessive when the system creates too many objects or the object graphs are too complicated, which we can analyze using the object allocations view of the profiler. We can fix this issue by simplifying long-living data structures or taking over GC by using off-heap memory allocation.[18]

The high-level idea behind moving some data to disk involves transferring infrequently used data. The MIT Advanced Data Structures course has several lectures on persistent data structures, which provide examples of moving data to disk.[19]

Latency Optimization Techniques

Latency or response time, the time from receiving the request to providing a response, is an odd one compared to other resources. We could argue it is not a resource but rather a measurement. However, when our primary focus is latency, looking at it as a resource and budgeting for it make sense.

For example, if a service call must finish within 100ms, we can budget each part of the code to respond within a given time period. In general, we can break the system into multiple parts in the pipeline and specify the latency limits for each part while monitoring the queue lengths. Next, let's look at the three primary methods to reduce latency.

Do Work in Parallel

If we can do work in parallel, we can reduce latency. It is worth noting that gains diminish quickly if work tasks are dependent on each other (Amdahl's law). One common use of this model is to push some work (e.g., I/O) to a different thread and respond to the user right away (a.k.a. asynchronous processing).

Reduce I/O

I/O is often thousands of times slower than memory operations (the operations hierarchy model). Reducing or eliminating I/O (e.g., using caching or prefetching) can improve latency significantly.

---

18. https://dzone.com/articles/heap-vs-heap-memory-usage

19. https://ocw.mit.edu/courses/6-851-advanced-data-structures-spring-2012/video_galleries/lecture-videos/

It is hard to hit the tens-of-a-microsecond range without eliminating I/O or pushing I/O to a different thread.

Admission Control

As discussed earlier regarding performance model 8, we can control latencies by monitoring queue lengths. We know from the queuing theory that latencies highly correlate with queue lengths. Therefore, we can control the average latency by monitoring queue lengths and applying back pressure to limit the intake of new requests.

Intuitive Feel for Performance

Although architects would run tests to verify their systems, it is possible to explore only some designs but not all. Given a target system, architects need to pick one to two potential architectures using an understanding of architecture models, technologies, performance models, and design concepts, which they can optimize further.

The first step is to use the knowledge about macro- and micro-level architectures to develop architectures, as we discuss in Chapters 5–10. To build an intuitive feel for the performance, we need to understand each architecture and choice using the eight performance models. Also, you need to do the same with any architecture case studies (e.g., http://highscalability.com). This exercise will deepen your understanding.

The second most important aspect is the real-life experience in solving performance problems. Take part in solving them when you can and talk to the people who have solved these problems and understand their root cause if this happens outside your team.

This book also discusses ideas for default choices when designing (e.g., how to implement a default service or default thread model). Understand the limits of the default choice and use defaults whenever possible. For example, a typical service can provide a latency range from a few milliseconds to hundreds of milliseconds; anything more than a second is usually high. A service provides throughput from tens to thousands of messages per second, while throughput beyond a few thousands requires careful handling. Understand the complex architecture choices in terms of variations from the default and the advantages and disadvantages of those choices. This book aims to explain those choices as much as possible.

Finally, the intuitive feel is practitioner knowledge and best imported in terms of mentors or apprenticeship models. Seek out and work with people who have that understanding and talk to them to comprehend deeply.

Leadership Considerations

Performance is a key factor in designing software systems. We need to think about performance alongside the leadership factors we talked about in Chapter 2.

First, when planning a system, we need to decide whether performance is something we can fix later or something we need to tackle immediately. Here are some questions and principles to help us decide:

- When is the best time to market? (Chapter 1, question 1)

- What is the skill level of the team? (Chapter 1, question 2)

- What is our system's performance sensitivity (Chapter 1, question 3)

- When can we rewrite the system? (Chapter 1, question 4)

- Does performance affect the users? (Chapter 1, principle 3)

When we are considering performance, the overall system design (macro architecture) is often more critical than specific service-level details. The reason is that it's usually easier to change service-level factors later. By the time we reach a point where we can redo the system, we can tackle both macro- and service-level performance issues. Therefore, we can put off performance concerns more easily than user experience (UX) worries.

If we need to focus on performance immediately, it often indicates a tough issue (Chapter 1, question 5). In this case, we should use principles 5 and 6 from Chapter 1: take time to design elements that are hard to change, but implement these changes slowly and eliminate uncertainties.

Moreover, decisions related to performance often involve a big-picture view and carry risks. As leaders, we need to make these decisions and shoulder these risks (Chapter 1, principle 4).

A gut feeling for performance is crucial for most architectural decisions. You can develop this by working closely with performance experts over time.

Summary

Performance is an inseparable factor in software architecture, and it dictates the limits of possibilities while designing the system.

To have an intuitive feel for the performance, we need to have a mental model (simply a representation of how something works) about the computer as it performs its work. Most performance limitations stem from the architecture, and we can use the eight models to make architectural choices at design time. Often an ideal design is impossible or requires complex programming, so our design needs to balance many aspects.

We can use the models presented in this chapter to optimize systems for CPU, memory, and performance. These models will help you think about and understand performance. For example, they will help you answer why the system is not using the leftover CPU. We also need to balance performance against other considerations. For example, when we look at throughput via MUU, the ideal system design includes operations that never block or wait (any blocking operation is handled asynchronously); operations are assigned to the same number of threads as the number of cores. However, often this ideal design is impossible or requires complex programming, so our design needs to balance many aspects.

These performance models are tools that we can use in design while crafting the architecture. We can use the models in this chapter to optimize systems for CPU, memory, and performance. The performance models, however, differ from performance analysis models because the former methods focus on the architecture rather than finding the bottlenecks. (See, for example, the Utilization Saturation and Errors [USE] method offered by Brendan Gregg at https://www.brendangregg.com/usemethod.html.)

It is apparent from those performance analysis models that much of the performance depends on your architecture, especially the thread model, which is hard to fix later. Hence, these performance models are not only tools for understanding performance, but tools that we can use in design while crafting the architecture. We see further applications of these models throughout the book, especially in Chapter 11.

We need to combine our understanding of performance with leadership considerations from Chapter 1 to find the design decisions that maximize our chance of success. Now we're ready to think about what users need from our system. In the next chapter, we dive into UX to better understand what this effort involves.

Understanding User Experience (UX)

I am no UX expert, so why am I talking about UX in an architecture book? Good UX goes beyond user interfaces (UIs) and applies to all the user touchpoints in a system. Furthermore, just like performance, UX always hovers around good architecture. It makes the architect's decisions easier and turns the odds of the system's success in our favor.

I will not write about how to create UIs because there are several good resources for that. My recommendation is *The Non-Designer's Design Book* by Robin Williams (Peachpit Press, 2015). Instead, I will focus on the other three touchpoints—APIs, configurations, and extensions—and, when it makes sense, point out how general design concepts extend to these use cases.

The main goal of this chapter is to build an appreciation for UX design among architects and to stress the need for professional expertise. Each application or system needs UX expertise in the team! The next section discusses how to think about UX while designing systems.

General UX Concepts for Architects

A perfect UX experience is like a perfect Omakase restaurant, where the chef chooses dishes for you without any input, knowing about you and anticipating what makes you happy. A perfect system anticipates what you want once you arrive there and guides you through it.

Unfortunately, we cannot get an Omakase chef to sit behind each request received in our systems. Instead, we use UX concepts to make each UI component intuitive, matching the user's mental model. Also, we can make recommendations to the user based on the current context.

With APIs, system configurations, and extensions, there is often no UI; hence, we often cannot make recommendations to the user. Users need to navigate, find, and use what they want. A good UX experience makes this process easy by making it evident, which is the right choice and by making the process of doing that as simple as possible.

For example, consider calling an API provided by our bookshop app. An example use case could be as follows: Users come to our web page, find the operation they need to call, and generate a sample client that they can download and use.

Let's walk through a few concepts or principles that help us to design a good UX.

Principle 1: Understand the Users

As you have undoubtedly heard, first, we need to understand the users. Doing so involves assessing their goals, their level of technical knowledge, their mental model of the system, and their typical workflow.

For example, our bookshop's users' mental model will likely follow a brick-and-mortar bookshop process, where users come in, browse, ask for help, select, pay, and take the book away. In addition, the users' actual workflow also involves providing shipping information, waiting for a book to arrive, and returning a book or talking to customer service if there is a problem. Understanding the mental model lets us anticipate our users and makes their experience seamless. This is also called the *principle of least astonishment*.

One of the best ways to understand the mental model of our users is to observe them in action. Our design approach of thinking deeply and implementing slowly creates many opportunities to observe and learn from users.

We should trace all user activities in the system in detail. Once the system is in production, we can learn much from those traces. Often, it is not useful to ask users because many behave differently than they themselves anticipate.

Also, based on their technical knowledge, users' expectations would be different. For example, in my experience, geeks love extension points, developers like samples and scripts, and nontechnical people prefer UIs. We need to anticipate and choose accordingly.

Commonly, a system has multiple types of users who require different UXs. There can be users who use the system to do different tasks, and new users may behave differently from experienced or expert users. Balancing those different UXs while leaving cues for different types of users is required. This makes UX design complex.

Principle 2: Do as Little as Possible

As we have discussed, we should implement only the necessary features. Everything you expose to the customer is a liability. For example, users get used to the features once offered, changing their mental model and expectations as needed. Even if you offer less-than-perfect experiences, removing them is tough because some users might be attached to those features. Furthermore, features create more opportunities for mistakes, diluting the focus on getting the UX right.

If there are widely used standards (e.g., security standards such as OAuth), we should adopt them. They save us the work of figuring out the UX, and usually, users already know well-known standards.

Principle 3: Good Products Do Not Need a Manual: Its Use Is Self-Evident

As discussed in several UX books such as *Don't Make Me Think* by Steve Krug (New Riders Publishing, 2006), users do *not* read the manual. As users, we all think we can figure it out. If we can't, then we decide (rightly) that the product is bad or inferior. If you attract customers and get them to invest in the application, they might later read the manual for advanced instructions but never for easy things and never at the early stage.

Hence, from the moment users arrive, we need to anticipate what they want and guide them either through explicit recommendations or subtle cues. For this process, the mental model and typical workflow we discussed previously are invaluable.

Principle 4: Think in Terms of Information Exchange

Users come to our system to get something done. The faster they can find what they need to do and do it, the happier they will be. If we can provide that UX without asking them anything, that's even better.

A few years back, I was flying on Northwest Airlines, and my baggage did not arrive at my destination. The next day I called to find out where the baggage was. When the call connected, before I told them anything, the automatic system told me where the baggage was and asked me to press 0 if I needed any more information. This was my perfect Omakase moment. Not only did it make me happy, but it also saved Northwest Airlines money in the long run and provided happy customers.

It is not always possible to guess the intent without input from users. Then, we need to ask the users

- For as little information as possible
- In the easiest way to get an answer

The first rule is to ask for as little information as possible, but if we can find a good default, we need to use it and not ask the users. If possible, remember the information or derive it from what we know about the users. For example, JVM, when starting up, looks at our hardware configurations and configures itself.

Also, never ask for the same information twice. If you must ask for information, ask in the easiest way possible to get an answer. For example, JVM lets the users set two modes: a server mode and an application mode. Instead of asking how to set the different configurations, JVM asks its users a question that they can easily answer and then derives the detailed configurations from the answer.

Another option is to use different UI controls (e.g., Date, Map, Photo) to make it easier for users to provide their input. If users need to learn more to make a good decision related to a configuration, then we must pick a default.

When you provide information to users, unless there is a performance concern, always provide more information and in a form users understand to help anticipate their needs. If users must get data from one call and pass it to another call, let them do that with the least amount of change to the data.

Principle 5: Make Simple Things Simple

When users first start using our system, they are often on the fence and unconvinced. The longer they use our system, however, the more comfortable they get and the more they feel invested in the system. Often, we are at a high risk of churn when a new user starts, but this risk lessens with time.

A user's first experiences with our system should be inviting and simple. We must really think through the UX and make the first few things the user does as easy as possible, removing any barriers and roadblocks. For example, a simple thing a user would want from a bookshop is to find a book. A search control should be prominent, easy to use, and when possible, we should be proactive by showing what we think they like even before issuing the search.

Similarly, with the book search API, letting users download a preconfigured client removes the burden of configuring it themselves. We can include a sample showing how to do that, making the first instructions simple.

With the first few things, we must educate users seamlessly and as deeply as possible. For example, Amazon Kindle does this elegantly in the first bootup and, in a few steps, explains how the UI works.

Principle 6: Design UX Before Implementation

Focusing on the UX before the architecture lets us zoom in to the details without bringing the underlying implementation to the picture. By digging into the UX early, we can avoid many costly changes, and the UX always needs a feedback cycle to get the system right. Keep in mind that this is a major factor in delaying the features, which is a recurring theme in this book.

Let us now explore how these principles apply to configurations, APIs, and extensions. As mentioned, I will not discuss UIs, which is a frequent subject in many books, because I have no hope of doing better.

UX Design for Configurations

Configurations let users change the behavior of a system. For example, the following is a YAML configuration file for a Go server:

```
# config.yml
server:
  host: 127.0.0.1
  port: 8080
  timeout:
    server: 30
    read: 15
    write: 10
    idle: 5
```

With configurations, we should start with the first principle of understanding the users and then use the second principle by doing as little as possible.

Avoid configurations as much as possible. As developers, when we cannot decide between two design choices and choose to create a configuration option, we pass the problem on to the users. This is a terrible idea: We are making the users' and solution architects' lives difficult. Because they know even less about how the system works than we do, users often can't decide well.

While we are creating configurations, the best option is to find a choice that works every time and to avoid the configuration. The next best strategy is to automatically make a choice, and the third best approach is to add a configuration parameter, setting a reasonable default. We must ask the question: Would users have a better context than me for choosing the configuration? If yes, configurations are needed; if no, we must avoid the configuration.

For example, let's consider the number of threads in a server. Who is best placed to set the number? We, the designers, understand how the server works a lot better than the end users. Thus, we need to set the number. Yes, the thread count depends on the load received by the server, but we can measure and adjust the thread count without passing it on to the user.

Sometimes, however, it is acceptable to ask the users. Consider a mobile app. Some users are mindful of mobile data usage, and some are not. We can ask, and if they say yes, we can automatically schedule downloads to times when mobile data is cheap. This configuration is good because it is about the users, and it is something they can answer meaningfully.

Next, let's explore applications of not forcing users to read the manual. All configurations must have sensible defaults. Then, if users do not understand the configuration, they can leave it alone. However, it is acceptable initially to ask users a few questions if they are straightforward questions, even if configurations should have defaults. For example, it is OK for an app to ask for a user's city, but even then, it should default to the most populated city.

For our configurations, unlike other applications, we can provide a manual. Poorly designed configurations can create much confusion. Always document a few sample values, possible ranges, and their meanings for the configuration, which we can add either to the configuration file or as helpful tips in the configuration UI.

A key aspect of understanding users is asking for configuration values in terms of things the users can answer readily, without making mental calculations to set the value. For example, do not ask for the number of maximum cache entries; instead, ask for the cache memory limit. Java asks us to choose an application mode, server versus client, instead of questions such as how much memory the application can use.

Finally, we should throw an error if we see an unknown configuration or the configurations failed to apply. Silent configuration errors are a source of many lost hours when debugging.

Always make it easy to find the current effective configuration after all configurations are applied. For example, a server can show the current active configurations (e.g., number of threads used, cache settings, and so forth) when it starts.

UX Design for APIs

Humans consume web pages and mobile apps, while computer programs (code) consume APIs. APIs enable the user system to work with other systems, creating value and great UXs. For example, the price API or recommendation API in the bookshop lets other sites show our books within their content (to get referral payments for the business they send our way).

APIs can be internal or public. Internal APIs connect different services in a system and create a tightly integrated program. At the same time, public APIs can become leaks. Data that gives you a competitive advantage can leak out through public APIs. It is critical to evaluate those aspects before opening the APIs.

Often, public APIs are an advanced use case and are usually enabled beyond the first minimum viable product (MVP). However, most systems have at least a few internal APIs, and most mobile apps have a backend that can later become an API.

We should start designing APIs early. Once an API is released and others have been built on top of it, changing it is tough. Although you might design and even build code for APIs, expose them to the users only when it is necessary. If possible, we should use the APIs internally before making them public because that enables us to find and fix problems.

Let's consider the first principle: understanding the user. APIs are used by other systems. Because other software developers use the APIs within code, we need to optimize APIs for software developers.

Considering the first, third, and fourth principles, a good API is easy to learn and hard to misuse, and at each step, the next step is apparent. By understanding the users, their mental model, and the workflow, we can achieve all three principles. For example, the API for the bookshop can closely follow a brick-and-mortar bookshop's mental model, making it easier for users to know what to do at each step.

Considering the second principle—do as few features as possible—useful APIs do one thing and do it well. If we are not sure, we should leave out the feature.

Considering the fifth principle, avoid boilerplate code. Think in terms of information and ask as little as possible. For example, if our users want to initiate a book search, all they should be doing is initializing a bookshop with configurations as a search call with keywords. This code snippet provides an example:

```
Bookshop bookShop = new Bookshop("/path/to/downloaded/config/file")
Book[] books = bookShop.search("Design Deeply")
bookShop.buy(book[5])
```

Note that we can avoid the configuration step by letting the users download a personalized configured client or a configuration file.

If a client has to send information back in follow-up calls, we need to create an object to enclose the information and ask the client to send it back. For example, in the previous code snippet, when buying a book, we can pass in the book object we received from the search without understanding the format of the book object.

If there are widely adopted standards for APIs, we should use them (e.g., OpenID, OpenAuth). Even when standards have room for improvement, it is a good idea to adopt the standards and, when possible, to provide an API on top to improve the UX. The best technology only sometimes wins, but standards that have momentum usually persist even when they are not the best technical answer. Bet on standards and adoption over technical correctness.

Most APIs work over HTTP, although they can also work over other transport protocols such as message queues, which we should choose based on the use case. Also, when possible, we should provide a client library to users. If we control both the client and the server, we have a lot more room for changes, and it simplifies the design. However, sometimes it takes work to provide client libraries because our APIs are used by clients running in many different environments.

Finally, we must version our APIs from the first design. Once the design is adopted, it is tough to ask customers to change their code, and the only way to update an API is to release new versions. While designing, we should communicate versioning in a manner that enables the standard load balancer to reroute requests to correct versions (e.g., via HTTP headers).

UX Design for Extensions

We use extensions when there are too many viable approaches within the problem scope, but the developers must choose one (for example, if the system accepts a date as a string). There are many acceptable date formats, and we can use extensions to support those formats.

Also, if the system can ingest data from many sources, we can leave extensions to enable new data sources. Activation functions and other extension points in the machine learning workflow are also good examples of extensions, where data scientists can use those extensions to change the behavior of the algorithms.

Well-designed extensions magnify the flexibility of a system; thus, they are powerful. If necessary, we can refactor the code to add extensions later. Indeed, it is a good idea to wait until we understand the use cases deeply.

Extension points are not limited to single-node apps or services. A service or cloud function can also act as an extension point. For example, Amazon uses cloud functions to extend the functionalities of its cloud platform, which is another good use of extensions.

The key challenge with extensions is that once they are written, they are hard to change. As a result, users are forced to live with older versions of the system, which in the long run, increases the maintenance costs of the system. If possible, the system should encourage users to contribute the extensions back to the code base, where the original developers can maintain them.

When we design extensions, we should decide what they can do. Just like a good API, a good extension also does one thing and does it well. We should define the input and output to control what our extensions can do. Input and output should be in terms of things the users understand, like APIs and configurations.

You must never expose internal data structures through extensions. Why? Because extensions break when we change internal data structures.

In most cases, few people write extensions, and our effort expanded on extensions should also reflect this. However, sometimes we engage in open source contributions through extensions, which help us attract a wider user population. In such cases, much more investment in extensions can be justified. A great example of this is iOS apps, which are extensions to iPhones and iPads. Apple was able to enlist thousands of developers to extend the iPhone.

Due to its central aspect, this book argues that system design should start with a UX design. My main goal in this chapter is twofold: to build an appreciation for UX design among architects and to emphasize the need for professional expertise. I highly recommend that your team include a world-class UX designer.

Leadership Considerations

UX, or user experience, is tricky to change once users have seen and used it. Changes can upset and confuse users and can even cause some systems to fail. So, we must pay careful attention to UX. This means we should always apply the principle of thinking deeply and implementing slowly when it comes to UX.

Common mistakes in many projects related to UX include

- Not having enough UX expertise on board

- Inviting UX experts too late in the process

- Overemphasizing the user interface (UI) while neglecting the UX of APIs, configurations, and extensions

- Overlooking suggestions from UX professionals

As a leader, you must ensure these mistakes don't occur. Given the importance of UX (see Chapter 2, Question 2), having UX expertise on the team is a must. If we lack UX skills, we'll likely face significant costs down the line.

Sometimes, UX experts might overly focus on the UI, neglecting the broader aspects of UX, such as APIs and configurations. Try to find experts who can handle broader UX aspects.

Another potential issue is that technical leaders may outline the overall UX and only ask UX experts to fine-tune the UIs. It's crucial to involve UX experts in broader UX discussions and heed their advice.

Furthermore, the iterative model we're proposing naturally incorporates UX:

- Principle 1: Drive everything from the user's journey.

- Principle 2: Use an iterative thin slice strategy.

- Principle 3: On each iteration, add the most value for the least effort to support more users.

Moreover, Chapter 2, Principle 5—Design deeply things that are hard to change but implement them slowly—provides many chances to watch and learn from the users. One of the best ways to grasp our users' mindset is to observe them in action. Hence, I recommend starting by designing the UX, which can prevent many expensive changes.

Summary

This chapter is much shorter than Chapter 3. That's because my aim isn't to teach you UX principles but to emphasize its importance and persuade you to bring UX expertise into the team early on and listen to their advice. Additionally, I want to stress the importance of UX for APIs, configurations, and extensions.

In this chapter, we discussed six UX principles that are useful for system architects. Then we talked about how those concepts apply to different touchpoints: configurations, APIs, and extensions. In the next few chapters, we'll look at the macro architecture.

Here are a few more key learnings from this chapter:

- A well-designed system interacts with its users seamlessly.

- A UX design plays a vital role in sound design, defining and fine-tuning user touchpoints: APIs, configurations, and extensions.

- A deep UX understanding helps us separate critical and nonessential features, which is a critical aspect of our design philosophy.

5

Macro Architecture: Introduction

Almost all modern systems run on multiple machines, which we call *distributed applications* or *systems*. Those systems need multiple machines due to the following reasons:

- Clients and data are distributed across many machines.
- A single machine can't handle the load of some applications.
- Systems need to talk to other systems as part of their functionality.

A distributed architecture must be able to store long-living data, sometimes across multiple requests; process user requests, either in response to direct requests or some kind of a trigger; and combine the state and logic to carry out the user requests efficiently. Macro architecture sees the systems as units (components or services) and their interactions.

Macro architecture includes building blocks (tools or middleware) that we can reuse in our design. Examples include databases, load balancers, message queues, and identity servers, which have stable open-source or vendor solutions. Reusing these tools can save us both time and money.

When we are building an application or a system, any functionality that we can't cover using architectural building blocks through reuse we implement as services: code running in the network, for instance. Services cover functionality that we can't reuse from a building block or that fix mismatches between the building blocks.

We can choose how to shape, lay out, and connect those services. For example, we can use service-oriented architecture (SOA) or resource-oriented architecture (ROA). I call this choice a *macro architecture strategy*. It dominates how we lay out and talk about macro architecture.

Furthermore, we define interfaces (APIs) between different parts of the system, which will increase our odds of being able to change parts without affecting the rest of the system.

As per the TOGAF architecture layers we explored in the first chapter, macro architecture falls under the umbrella of information systems architecture. When we're designing the macro architecture, numerous designs are feasible, and it's the business context that determines the most suitable architecture. As we've noted before, selecting the best architecture demands sound judgment.

Our architecture should handle several concerns. The first is that different services need to work together, which I call *coordination*. Next is how the overall system can have a meaningful and consistent state. The third concern is handling the system's security, and the fourth is ensuring the system is highly available and can scale to the required load.

Let's first explore different approaches for building distributed applications that evolve over time and then explore the building blocks. Chapters 6–9 handle the rest of the macro architecture topics, and Chapter 10 discusses how microservices affect the architecture.

History of Macro Architecture

One of the first solutions for building distributed apps was remote procedure calls (RPCs), where users annotate certain procedure calls or methods as remotely callable, and the RPC runtime generates a server and client. Most Linux services are written this way.

First, RPC implementations used custom protocols where communication between server and client happens using custom binary protocols. That protocol eventually moved to XML and JSON, exchanged on top of HTTP. In recent years, the trend has reverted to binary protocols, such as thrift and RPC.

The first distributed apps were monoliths, where a server receives the request, does all processing, and returns a response. For example, our bookshop, implemented as a monolith, renders UIs, handles logic, and talks to databases. If we need to do more things with that implementation, we need a faster machine, which is harder to scale. Monoliths, however, are harder to understand and make it difficult for a team to work together.

Next came the three-tier architecture, which arranges applications into three tiers: a web tier for the UI, an application tier for the logic, and a database tier for data storage. Soon, we extended three tiers to *N* tiers, so now all modern architectures use *N*-tier architectures.

The next evolution happened to the programming model. Building on object-oriented programming (OOP), which gained popularity as a programming model, remote object frameworks extended RPC to remote objects that can be instantiated, discovered, invoked, managed, and destroyed. Among the examples are Java RMI and .NET DCOM. However, remote object frameworks had a fundamental limitation: although all services written in the same programming language could talk to each other, it was hard to speak across multiple programming languages. We call the ability to communicate across different programming languages *interoperability*.

Organizations often need to communicate with each other as part of their day-to-day operations. For example, any airline needs to talk to all other airlines regardless of what platform they use. Likewise, the bookshop needs to talk to payment APIs. Eventually, the need for interoperability gave rise to CORBA (Common Object Request Broker Architecture) (see Figure 5.1).

CORBA is an interoperable distributed object framework that enables users to create remote objects that can be instantiated, discovered, invoked, managed, and destroyed. CORBA supports multiple programming languages, and objects created in different languages can talk to each other and work as a single system.

CORBA failed as a platform, yet it made several innovations. First, it defined an interface definition language (IDL), a platform-independent way to describe service interfaces. Second, it enabled communication between different systems using message-level interoperability, agreeing to use the same message format.

Although CORBA was the most technically advanced platform ever built, it was hard for users to understand. Its API was a nightmare! A simple service call needed hundreds of lines. There were only so many developers who could handle the complexity, which led to its limited adoption.[1]

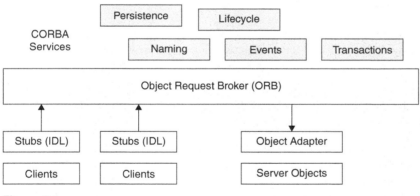

Figure 5.1
CORBA architecture.

Web services came next, which are a simple version of CORBA in many ways: they are CORBA without objects. Web services replace distributed objects with RPC and all message formats with XML, which makes it easy to understand and debug. Also, web services had the seal of approval from the top two enterprise technology companies at the time, Microsoft and IBM.

---

1. Read "The Rise and Fall of CORBA" at https://queue.acm.org/detail.cfm?id=1142044.

With web service success over CORBA, we see a simple design with minimum features overshadowing and replacing a complex and feature-rich system, a common theme you will find across the book. When we're building systems, simplicity often trumps more accurate but complex systems.

Building on top of web services, SOA formalized the former. According to SOA, distributed apps are built using coordinating services to fulfill the use case. Each service includes operations, where each operation represents a "verb" in the use case. For example, in the bookshop, the services would be called *search, buy, fulfill,* and *return*. A user would search for books and then buy them, which would trigger a fulfillment and, optionally, a return.

ROA proposed an alternative way to arrange services, which was called *resources*. Those resources represent "nouns" in the use case. For example, in our bookstore, we have *BookCatalog* and *Order*. Each resource supports the actions PUT, POST, GET, and DELETE. Users use GET operations to find a book, which they buy by creating an order through a PUT action, and then they can return it by deleting the order through the DELETE action.

Unlike before, ROA did not replace SOA. It continues as a competing yet valid way to create modern architectures. Some use cases are a natural fit for SOA, whereas others are a natural fit for ROA.

Modern Architectures

Modern architectures follow an *N*-tier setup, where each tier is a separate layer dealing with distinct issues. For instance, the layers could include a database layer, a services layer, a coordination layer, and an API and load-balancing layer. Different combinations of layers can be used.

Modern architectures can use either SOA or ROA. Although the previous concepts have remained mostly unchanged, implementations have evolved. For example, communication protocols have progressed from HTTP plus XML to HTTP plus JSON, thrift, protocol buffers, GRPC, and HTTP2.

Years ago, systems moved from binary protocols to text protocols such as XML and JSON over HTTP. Now we see that performance-sensitive use cases are going back to binary protocols. Although not well received when concepts were introduced, binary protocols are returning, likely helped by the wider familiarity of the services' architectural concepts. My recommendation is to start with HTTP JSON as the default solution and depart from that only if there is a compelling reason to do so.

Important updates to design tools are WebSocket and HTTP2. These protocols enable two-way (pull and push) communication between the client and server. Figure 5.2 shows the outline of components in modern architecture.

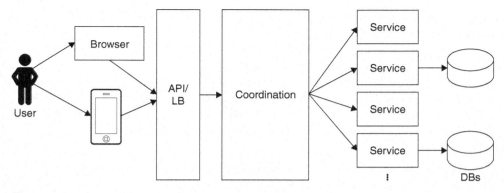

Figure 5.2
Outline of modern software architecture components.

As the figure depicts, a typical software architecture stores the data in a database and implements the logic as stateless services. When a user sends a request, either through a web page, a mobile app, or via a scheduled task, the coordination layer uses the services to complete the use case. Coordination layers can also include details such as caching. Before that, the API and load-balancing (LP) layer handle the high availability (HA), routing, scale, rate limiting, and security. We can also engage middleware services such as service authoring and management platforms, message brokers, workflow systems, and identity and access management (IAM). When we're designing, the primary challenge is to handle the state and scaling. As such, the three key nonfunctional requirements of the architecture are HA, scale, and security.

The macro architecture dictates how those services and middleware work together to deliver the application's use cases. This and the next chapter describe different considerations in building such an architecture. Chapter 11 discusses how to implement individual services.

Our discussion breaks the macro architecture into four problems: how to design the coordination, how to keep a consistent state while performing coordination, how to handle security, and how to add HA and scale. The following chapters focus on each topic.

Macro Architectural Building Blocks

There are many architectural building blocks. Macro architecture reuses those building blocks, reuses their implementations when possible, and uses services to implement the missing parts. Covering the building blocks in detail would require many books. Following is a just quick outline with suggested references for more information.

As architects, we need to be aware of these tools and keep track of newly available tools. These tools are available as open-source projects or vendor-provided proprietary software.

Additionally, most architecture building blocks are now available in the cloud or as APIs. Following are some of the common types of tools:

- **Data Management**

  Databases: Store tabular data and index it, enabling us to query the data (often using SQL). Relational databases also support transactions. NoSQL (columnar) databases support rich data formats (e.g., JSON) but only relaxed versions of transactions. Both open-source (e.g., MySQL, PostgreSQL) and commercial (e.g., MSSQL, Oracle) production-grade implementations are available.

  Distributed caches: Provide a large virtual cache that's partitioned between many nodes. Hazelcast and Apache Ignite are two widely used implementations.

  Registries: Usually, a shared repository of information between different parts of the system, registries can hold diverse types of information such as configurations, service or API descriptions, and domain names. Different implementations (e.g., etcd; see http://etcd.io) are available based on the type of information stored in the system.

- **Routers and Messaging**

  Load balancers: Sit in front of a server or a system and route or modify the traffic. We often use load balancers for HA and scalability. Hardware (e.g., F5) and software (e.g., NGINX) implementations are available. We discuss them more in Chapter 9.

  API managers: Securely expose services outside the trust domain while managing security, subscriptions, and other quality-of-service aspects. Several open-source (e.g., WSO2 API Manager) and commercial (e.g., Google Apigee) implementations are available.

  Enterprise service buses (ESBs): Let applications connect different systems and organizations to enable them to work together by translating messages and resolving differences (e.g., timing) between them. Several open-source (e.g., WSO2 ESB) and commercial (e.g., Mule ESB) implementations are available.

  Message brokers: Support distributed message queues and publish/subscribe (Pub/Sub) patterns in a persistent manner, where messages are deleted after the process acknowledges the message. We use the message queue for reliable asynchronous processing when we want to distribute tasks across multiple threads of executions without one task having to wait on the other tasks to finish. We use the Pub/Sub pattern to notify interested parties about events. Both open-source (e.g., ActiveMQ, RabbitMQ) and commercial (e.g., IBM MQ, TIBCO) production-grade implementations are available. Apache Kafka provides a fast and scalable Pub/Sub implementation with more relaxed guarantees than classical message brokers.

- **Executors**

  Workflow systems: Support the execution of long-running tasks, writing all the steps in the execution to storage, which enables us to restore or rewind a task as needed.

A workflow can execute for years, even outlasting computers that run them. Sample systems are Apache Ode and Kamunda.

MapReduce systems: Let us process large amounts of data as batch tasks. Apache Spark is the production-grade implementation used exclusively.

Containers/VM managers: Control large collections of containers or virtual machines (VMs) deployed on top of real hardware. Most modern systems are deployed on top of container orchestration systems because they provide better control. Kubernetes is the widely used solution for containers, and VMware is widely used for VMs.

- **Security**

IAM servers: Carry out most of the security needs of an organization, including user management, authentication, authorization, issuing of tokens, single sign-on, and so forth. Several open-source (e.g., WSO2 Identity Server), commercial (e.g., Centrify), and cloud (e.g., Asgardeo, Auth0) production-grade implementations are available.

- **Communication**

Distributed hash tables DHTs): Create an efficient overlay network connecting N nodes to provide routing with $\log(N)$ hops. Although DHTs are used as part of the system, no widely used production-grade implementations are available.

Gossip architectures: Enable us to synchronize data among a large number of nodes, while providing limited guarantees. This idea is used with many NoSQL systems. No widely used production-grade implementations are available.

Tree of responsibility patterns: Distribute a task among nodes arranged like a tree, carry out the task, and collect the results. The idea is used widely, but implementation depends on the specific use case.

Distributed coordination systems: Provide a wide range of primitives used for multiple nodes to work together (e.g., distributed locks, barriers, and signaling between threads). Apache ZooKeeper (open source) and Redis are widely used production-grade implementations.

- **Other**

Transaction managers: Enable systems to carry out Atomicity, Consistency, Isolation, and Durability (ACID) transactions. Because systems can carry out most transactions through a database, we need transaction managers only for more complex use cases, which we discuss in Chapter 7. Atomikos (open source) is a widely used production-grade transaction manager implementation. Application servers such as WebLogic, IBM WebSphere, and JBoss also include transaction managers.

In addition, we can use many libraries and frameworks such as LMAX Disruptor. Unfortunately, covering them is beyond the scope of this book.

Leadership Considerations

Macro architecture is the place where the most crucial decisions are made. Think of it as laying the foundation when building a house. While you can make some modifications later, your options are mostly set once the foundation is in place. Hence, careful consideration is necessary. But at the same time, you don't always want to construct a house that can accommodate the needs of three generations, recognizing that sometimes a rebuild will be necessary.

Most of our leadership questions and principles apply here:

> Question 1: When is the best time to market?
>
> Question 2: What is the skill level of the team?
>
> Question 3: What is our system's performance sensitivity?
>
> Question 4: When can we rewrite the system?
>
> Question 5: What are the hard problems?

Questions 1, 2, and 4 introduce the business context and question how much we want to address in the first attempt and what we might postpone for future redesigns. Questions 3 and 5 prompt us to understand the system. For instance, if the system requires exceptional performance, macro architecture needs to factor that in.

The following three principles apply for macro architecture:

> Principle 4: Make decisions and absorb the risks.
>
> Principle 5: Design deeply things that are hard to change but implement them slowly.
>
> Principle 6: Eliminate the unknowns and learn from evidence by working on hard problems early and in parallel.

Principles 5 and 6 highlight one of the key challenges of macro architecture: deciding the right level of detail to consider. We need to see enough details to ensure the macro architecture is valid, but we don't want to get bogged down in them. Business context introduces another layer of uncertainty into the system, and managing these two types of uncertainties calls for sound judgment. Principle 6 encourages us to make those decisions and accept the risks when the team doesn't have enough information to make the decision.

Macro architecture will aim to boost efficiency by handling everything from one spot, like a service, and reusing it. Here, we need to recall principle 7: Understand the trade-offs between coherence and flexibility in the software architecture. Striving for excessive reuse of certain components might lead to more expenses if the cost of depending on it outweighs the cost of building it again. (Refer to Chapter 2 for a more detailed explanation.)

Finally, choosing building blocks (tools) is a key architectural decision. As discussed, we implement functionality gaps left after choosing the tools using services. Choosing the right building blocks can significantly speed up the time to market. Following are some rules of thumb for making that decision.

My first recommendation is to be biased toward using tools as much as possible. They can save time and money and also give us a stable and better-performing system. Furthermore, if tools are backed by active communities or thriving companies, they will evolve, saving us the time and effort required to improve their functionality.

Several risks are associated with using a tool. If we need improvements to the tool, especially if not supported, as mentioned previously, those improvements are either impossible or will take a lot of time. You need to be sure the tool in its current form can support your use case. Also, sometimes a tool can be a bad fit because it can barely support your use case. This kind of mismatch often leads to performance problems and affects your design.

We need to always start by considering the tool as an unknown (principle 6 in Chapter 2). We should explore and verify that the tool can support the immediate use cases up to rewrite or print (question 4 in Chapter 2). Dig deep into the tool's documentation and use cases and talk to developers and other users who are making use of the same tool. This verification needs to include performance. Also, if an unexpected problem happens, we need to make sure that we have a way to dig into the tool, find the problem, and at least create a workaround, which usually requires either building expertise within the internal team or coming to a financial agreement with a company or a developer who knows the tool well.

When choosing tools, try to choose tools built using accepted standards. Examples are SQL, HTTP, WebSockets, HTTP2, JSON, XML, protocol buffers, JMS, and AMQP. Acceptable standards have wider user bases, which enables vendors to invest more money in building the tools and also creates multiple organizations that can collaborate and pool their resources. Well-known standards make hiring developers easier. Furthermore, tools built on peak standards often tend to be mature and stable.

When using tools that are not based on accepted standards, use them in a way that, if needed, they can be removed or replaced. For the same reason, I prefer using tools as libraries instead of frameworks because the latter is often hard to remove later.[2] Even so, this is not always possible. With frameworks, use the tool after understanding the rewrite point (question 4 in Chapter 2). This may be a risky decision, but as leaders, we need to make it without passing it on (principle 4 in Chapter 2).

When we build a system, using some tools such as the operating system, TCP/IP, and HTTP is unavoidable. These tools are stable enough to be disregarded as a risk but nevertheless still carry the same risks. We should be bold in using a good tool while minimizing the risks by eliminating unknowns (principle 6 in Chapter 2).

---

2. See https://www.gwern.net/docs/cs/2005-09-30-smith-whyihateframeworks.html.

Summary

In this chapter, we discussed the history of macro architecture, the state of the art, and best practices.

As primary considerations in a macro architecture, we looked at coordination, state, security, HA, and scale.

Most of our leadership questions and principles can help us with macro architecture.

We also discussed building blocks (tools) that we can use to build our system and how to choose them.

In Chapters 6–9, we handle the rest of the macro architecture topics. In Chapter 10, we discuss how microservices affect the architecture.

6

Macro Architecture: Coordination

A modern architecture includes services, databases, APIs, libraries, and Software as a Service (SaaS), and coordination makes everything work together. For example, when a user buys a book, the system processes the payment, prepares the book to be shipped, sets up delivery, and responds to the customer. Coordination decides the flow that connects the different parts together.

Depending on the use case, coordination can be simple or complex. Coordination code talks to many parts of the systems over the network as it does I/O operations (disk and network read/writes). If one service is a major bottleneck or if the system is performance-sensitive, we need to design the coordination layer carefully. There are several ways to create this design

Approach 1: Drive Flow from Client

The first approach is to put the coordination logic into the user's client, which is either the browser or the mobile app in most cases. The presentation "Domain Service Aggregators: A Structured Approach to Microservice Composition" gives an example of this approach, as shown in Figure 6.1.[1]

---

1. https://www.infoq.com/presentations/domain-service-aggregator/

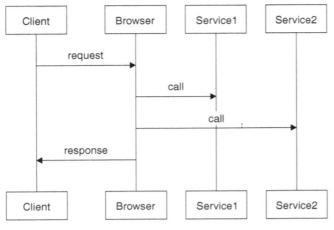

Figure 6.1
Microservice composition from the client.

This approach is simple, because we do not need a separate coordination layer, yet it has several drawbacks.

With this approach, the client triggers many service calls to the rest of the system. If the client is behind a slow wide area network (WAN), this adds high latency (a mobile network is the most common cause for this issue). In contrast, if we place the coordination layers inside the same data center as the services, the client triggers the first call, and the subsequent calls happen within the data center. This approach has much better latency than the former approach. For example, if a WAN has a 300ms latency and the intranet call is 20ms, coordination with three services (driven from the client) takes 900ms but would take only 340ms otherwise.

Furthermore, because the coordination logic runs in the client's device, an attacker could change the flow, creating a security breach. For example, with the bookshop's loan approval process running on my laptop, using this root access and some serious OS-level code, an attacker with unsavory credit can change the process to bypass loan checks.

Approach 2: Use Another Service

We can write a service that receives the client's request and then carry out the coordination. If the coordination finishes quickly (e.g., within a few seconds), this is a strong choice.

The primary disadvantage of using another service for coordination is that a lot depends on the performance of the service. Because the coordination service makes many service calls, the simplest server architectures such as the thread-per-request model do not provide good performance, and implementing a nonblocking asynchronous style service is complicated. If you choose to write code to do asynchronous calls, make sure you have a few team members who have done it before.

Approach 3: Use Centralized Middleware

Several middleware solutions are optimized for writing coordination code. We discuss three options here:

- First is an enterprise service bus (ESB), such as WSO2 ESB and Mule ESB. They support writing the highly optimized, nonblocking coordination logic using a higher-level integration language with first-class support for invoking other services. This option provides superior performance.

- The second uses a workflow such as Business Process Execution Language (BPEL) or Business Process Modeling and Notation (BPMN). Workflows let you specify the coordination logic using a workflow language such as BPEL or BPMN. They typically support transactions as a first-class concept. They also support efficient nonblocking service invocations and are specifically designed for long-running coordinations that might run for days or years. Workflows can recover from failures because they save their state at each step of the execution and will reverse the flow and call compensation operations if failures happen. They support compensation as first-class entities, where we can provide undo operations. However, for simple use cases, they can be too heavy, too slow, and sometimes too expensive.

- The third alternative, the Ballerina programming language, is optimized for coordination logic. The choice really lies in balancing the pros and cons of the first two approaches: writing your own service or using workflows.

A key advantage of centralized coordination middleware is first-class support for asynchronous calls, where we call a service but can do other work until the response comes. This approach provides superior latency and performance. If you are using this approach, send data as early as possible and ask for information as late as possible (don't ask for information but get the information holder to send it proactively). As mentioned in Chapter 3, this maximum is called "Send Early, Receive Late, Don't Ask but Tell."

For example, say we call three APIs and then process and combine the results. This principle says that we should issue API calls before processing any results, increasing the chance that the results are available when they are needed and reducing the probability of having to wait.

Approach 4: Implement Choreography

Driving the flow from a central place is not the only way to coordinate multiple partners to carry out some work. For example, in a dance, no one person directs the performance. Instead, each dancer follows who is close and synchronizes with them. Choreography applies the same idea to business processes.

A typical choreography implementation includes an event-driven system, where each participant in the process listens to different events and carries out their individual part.

Each action generates asynchronous events, which trigger participants downstream. We can use programming environments like RxJava or Node.js to build event-driven systems.

For example, let's assume that a loan process includes a request, a credit check, another outstanding loans check, manager approval, and a decision notification. Figure 6.2 shows the flow of information using choreography. The request is placed in a queue; it then is picked up by the next actor, who puts the results in the next queue; and the process continues until it completes.

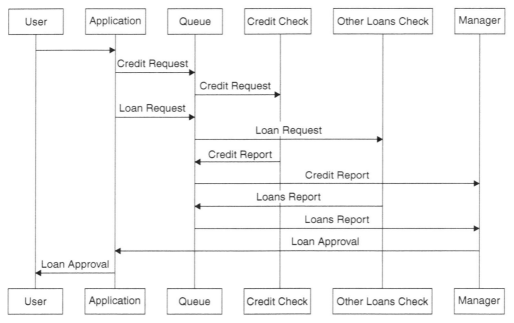

Figure 6.2
A typical choreography implementation.

It is important to note that although we depict it as a sequence diagram, any independent events can happen parallel with choreography.

As the figure shows, choreography is like a dance. Both are complicated and need practice for correct execution. For example, on one hand, the programmer does not know if or when the process finishes, if an error occurs, or if the process is stuck. Choreography needs extensive monitoring to track progress and to recover or to notify us about an error.

On the other hand, the choreography creates loosely coupled systems, which is its main advantage. For example, you can add a new actor to the process without changing other actors and often without changing the process. You can find more information about event streams and choreography in "Scaling Microservices with an Event Stream."[2]

---

2. https://www.thoughtworks.com/insights/blog/scaling-microservices-event-stream

Leadership Considerations

Compared with other topics, decisions in this area are relatively straightforward.

I advise starting with either "Drive flow from the client" or "Another service." In most cases, one of these two options should be sufficient.

Two frequent missteps include implementing workflows or integration tools too early, or conversely, avoiding the shift to them even when necessary. All four initial architecture questions from Chapter 2 should influence your decision. Your choice should consider factors such as timing (questions 1 and 4), performance (question 3), and the skill level of your team (question 2).

Summary

In this chapter, we discussed several means for implementing coordination. You may have noticed that I suggested only single-level depth in the call tree of coordination, and that is intentional. Having a low depth simplifies the code, makes it readable, and makes it easier to debug. Table 6.1 summarizes the advantages and disadvantages of each approach.

Table 6.1   Comparison of Coordination Approaches

Coordination Approach	Pros	Cons	When to Use
Drive flow from client	Simple coordination code is part of the client.	There are performance and security concerns.	With app using simple coordination logic.
Another service	You can implement it with the existing language and tools. It fits well with the microservice architecture.	It offers limited performance. Performant nonblocking implementation is complex.	In simple cases when performance is not a major concern.
Centralized middleware	It provides high-performant service calls.	You need to learn a different DSL or language; it is a poor fit with the microservice architecture.	In moderately complex cases.
Workflows (choreography)	It provides high-performant service calls and support for long-running executions.	It is too heavy for simple cases.	In long-running or complex logic.

7

Macro Architecture: Preserving Consistency of State

Why Transactions?

Transactions help us avoid data inconsistencies. For example, many nodes participate in coordination logic. Due to scale or high availability, we might keep multiple copies of some data points whose values can drift while updates momentarily happen. Moreover, one of those nodes, networks, any outside dependencies, or communication can fail, stopping the complete execution or creating long-lasting inconsistencies. A well-designed app must never end up in an unexpected state regardless of the challenges.

Inconsistencies can take a second form also. Even running an app has side effects. For example, the bookshop app charges money from the customer to deliver books. Also, it updates its internal data storage (for example, changing an inventory table to represent how many books are left in the store). In the app's specification, we define how these side effects happen. For example, we must ship the book if we have charged the account, and we must not reduce inventory without selling a book.

A well-designed app never deviates from its specifications. This section discusses how we handle these cases. We can achieve this goal by analyzing all failure conditions and writing code to ensure the application behaves according to the specification.

For example, we charge for the book, and then we ship it. If shipping fails, we retry the transaction, and if it fails too, we return the money (void the transaction if by bank card) and notify the customer. If any of the responses to failure fail, we need to handle that issue too. However, addressing this issue is easier said than done because it requires complicated code. For example, if the service fails while we are performing the shipping operation, when the system recovers, we might not know the outcome of the shipping operation. Log-based recovery algorithms can handle similar conditions, even after a failure, but they are complex. Compensating for failures and for the responses to failures is also complex. Developers, most likely including you and me, may not get this right for complex scenarios and may spend weeks and months writing the same code and troubleshooting it.

Transactions enable us to avoid this complexity. Transactions provide four guarantees when multiple operations are performed at the same time:

- **Atomic:** All side effects produced by the operations occur or none at all.
- **Consistency:** Data storage goes only from one consistent state to another.
- **Isolation:** The outcomes of operations from two interleaved transactions are as if two transactions happen consecutively.
- **Durability:** When committed, the transaction stays committed.

Typically, these guarantees are supported as part of the database, which does the hard work of handling all the complexities. Using transactions, developers can focus on the business logic without having to worry about failure. In 1998, Jim Gray, the inventor of transactions, won the Turing award, which spotlights the importance of transactions. E-commerce and most enterprise use cases would not have been possible without transactions.

Why Do We Need to Go Beyond Transactions?

When we want to design a system, how can we build a system on top of transactions? We know that databases support transactions, which we can use with database clients. We also know that when data is changed or read, it can be inconsistent. To avoid inconsistencies, we can carry out each read and write within a transaction; then data will be consistent.

However, users also use our applications through mobile or web applications. Due to security reasons, mobile or web applications can't talk to the database directly. They need to talk to a service, which talks to a database and carries out our transactions. For example, if a user wants to buy a book, that user indicates that desire in the web app, which talks to a service, which, in turn, communicates with a database.

The most trivial way of handling transactions is to put all logic into a single service and call that service, which carries out the transaction. However, this approach goes against the typical service-based architecture (e.g., SOA or ROA) we discussed in Chapter 5.

Instead, we can break the code into multiple services and coordinate the execution to call those services as discussed in Chapter 6. To coordinate the transaction across multiple services, we use a transaction manager (e.g., Atomikos). We first initialize the transaction with the transaction manager and talk to each service as needed, passing references to the transaction. We later ask the transaction manager to commit the translation. The transaction manager coordinates between the different participants in the transaction and safely completes it.

If we use a single database for all data, although we use a transaction manager, overhead is limited. The reason is that, behind the curtain, there is only one transaction-aware participant (the database in the transaction). This is a common scenario. Figure 7.1 shows a sample setup.

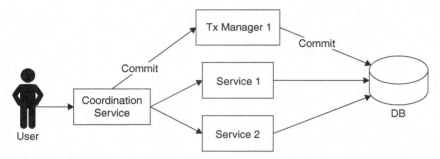

Figure 7.1
Multiple services using the single database as transaction participant.

If there is more than one participant in the transaction (e.g., multiple databases, JMS broker, and other transaction-aware resources), the transaction manager must carry out a distributed transaction using the two-phase commit protocol (see https://en.wikipedia.org/wiki/Two-phase_ commit_protocol). Distributed transactions are complex and heavy. Using distributed transactions significantly reduces the performance of the applications. Transactions have a limited scale, typically limited to hundreds of transactions per second. When high performance is needed, we must avoid or limit the use of transactions.

Furthermore, in some cases, not all parties can take part in a transaction. For example, often, we cannot ask the customer to be part of the transaction. Typically, we must accept the request from the customer and carry out the transaction. If it succeeds or fails, we notify the customer and carry out necessary corrective action if needed. For example, if the book the customer ordered is missing from our inventory, we can't reverse the order using a transaction.

We can't ask every customer to be part of a transaction. Instead, we need to talk to the customer and return the money. In other words, we must combine transaction and nontransaction codes. To keep the system's consistency under these conditions, we may have to go beyond transactions.

Going Beyond Transactions

There are two broad approaches to going beyond transactions: The first is to redefine the problem to require lesser guarantees, and the second is to use compensations. These are complex techniques, and as with many other complex techniques, we must use them only when necessary.

Approach 1: Redefining the Problem to Require Lesser Guarantees

The idea here is to figure out a way to resolve complex situations. For example, in the bookstore, we can choose first to ship the book and then deduct the money. If the logic fails and we can't decide what happened, we can take the hit and not charge the customer. When failure is rare, it is often cheaper to not charge than to build a system that supports distributed transactions with the required throughput. When you take this approach, whenever possible, the system should bear the cost of inconsistencies, not the user.

In other cases, the user can't tell the difference between the weaker guarantees or accept them. For example, on a social media site, as long as I see all my activities and other activities that are causally related and happen before my activities, I can't detect inconsistencies (this is called "read your writes"). When we evaluate consistency from the user's point of view, we can relax the need for consistency. Several of these models are described under client-centric consistency models (see https://en.wikipedia.org/wiki/Consistency_model#Client-centric_consistency_models).

Another simple idea is to provide a button for users to forcefully refresh the page if they can tell that it is outdated. Also, sometimes eventual consistencies or timeouts are sufficient where we can bite the bullet and settle for a lesser consistency; for example, Werner Vogel's post, "Eventually Consistent" (http://www.allthingsdistributed.com/2007/12/eventually_consistent.html) is a good starting point.

It is important to communicate these assumptions and to associate costs with stakeholders and to agree on the limited guarantees provided by the system. An architect must not leave lesser guarantees as a surprise to stakeholders or to the users. Rather, you need to communicate and agree about limited guarantees early and then set the right expectations for the users through the right UX design.

Approach 2: Using Compensations

As the famous post "Starbucks Does Not Use Two-Phase Commit" describes, the normal world works without transactions.[1] For example, baristas at Starbucks do not wait until your transaction completes. Instead, they handle multiple customers at the same time, compensating for any errors explicitly. You can do the same if you are willing to do a bit more work. The key idea is that if an action fails, you can compensate.

It is important to understand that what transactions do is also a form of compensation, and compensation can be complex because it can also fail. However, when the following three conditions are true, we can implement compensation with limited effort. When these conditions are not true, compensation is complex, and we need to use distributed transactions.

---

1. https://news.ycombinator.com/item?id=7995130

Often, we can design most systems such that they satisfy these three conditions. Let's explore them in detail:

- **Condition 1:** Each individual operation can be verified.

- **Condition 2:** The system does not have writes or side effects that cause operations to depend on a read from a mutable state.

- **Condition 3:** We can handle the failure or take compensative actions.

The first condition, the individual operations, can be verified if any of the following conditions are true:

- The operation is carried out as a transaction. This is a local transaction that happens with a single resource, not a distributed transaction.

- The operation is idempotent. If we repeat the operation with the same data, no additional side effects occur. For example, if our shipping service ships only once for a single order, even if we call the shipping service multiple times with the same data, it is idempotent. The implementation remembers processed requests and ignores any duplicates.

- We can check the status of the operation via an API call. For example, if the courier service lets us check the status of the shipping operation and we can't decide what happened, we can call this API.

In condition 2, side effects mean that the operation changes something significantly. For example, a shipping operation has the side effect of shipping something to a customer, or as another example, charging a customer takes money from the customer. To understand the second condition, the read-dependent writes and operations, let's consider the following example:

```
count = readInventory(..)
If count > 0:
writeToInventory(..)
chargeCustomer(..)
fulfilOrder(..)
return ..
Else
handOffToPartner(..)
return ..
```

Here, we read the item count, and the next operation depends on this. Consider that there are two transactions happening, and both have read the item count. If the first transaction checks the condition and updates the item count to zero, to enforce the isolation condition of transactions, the database must roll back the second transaction.

To enforce isolation, the database needs to keep track of reads and writes that happen in transactions, and if two transactions are in conflict, it commits only one. Handling this situation without the help of transactions is complicated. Hence, it is difficult to use compensation to handle similar cases where the next write depends on a read because you will end up implementing a significant portion of the database while doing so.

The third condition states that it is possible to carry out compensative action. When all three conditions are met, we can use compensation. Table 7.1 summarizes when we can use compensation. Batching means collecting the operations and carrying them out together as a single transaction if possible.

Table 7.1   Using Compensation

	No External Operations	Only Operations Without Side Effects	Has Operations with Side Effects
Read operations only	No transaction needed	No transaction needed	Use compensation
Write operations only	Batch them and execute or use compensation	Batch them and execute or use compensation	Batch them and execute or use compensation
Writes do not depend on read operations	Batch them and execute or use compensation	Batch them and execute or use compensation	Batch them and execute or use compensation
Writes depend on reads	Need transactions	Need transactions	Need transactions

When we use compensation or batch operations, we need to make sure all the steps are carried out. We can use databases or message queues to remember partial steps and then carry them out. If the second condition is true, it is OK to repeat some of the operations when compensating. If transactions are needed, the best choice is to use workflows.

This section discussed three conditions that we need to meet when using compensation and how those conditions can be handled. The article "Life Beyond Distributed Transactions: An Apostate's Opinion" by Pat Helland (https://queue.acm.org/detail.cfm?id=3025012) provides a discussion of these techniques.

Best Practices

Here are a few best practices we can adhere to when working with transactions:

- Many distributed applications have one to two service calls for each user request. In this case, it may be possible to avoid the coordination layer.

- When possible, go for lesser guarantees. Consider the failure when transactions are not there and ask if you can gracefully recover from that. For example, a video streaming service needs to use transactions for payment, but a movie stream does not need them. The same goes for the online bookshop; it does not need to use transactions while browsing books.

- When possible, make service operations or API calls idempotent. This makes the implementation of transaction-like scenarios simple.

- Define the scope of the transaction to be as restrictive as possible. If possible, limit it to a single service and avoid distributed transactions.

- Put operations that read and write data into the same service call when possible. For example, if we rewrite the code so that we can check for inventory availability, reduce it in the database and return the value as one operation. This practice removes the read-dependent write due to inventory.

My recommendation is to use a transactions manager with one participant as the default solution and go for complex solutions as needed.

Let's discuss these practices with a working example. As an example of transaction choices, let's consider several design choices for the bookstore. A user needs to search for books and wants to add selected books to the shopping cart. When the user clicks Buy, we need to check our inventory, charge the user, and schedule delivery. Let's assume that we store the shopping cart in the user's browser. First, searching for books reads only read-only data, so the catalog can be excluded from all transactions. Here are our design choices:

- **Design 1:** We can put checking the inventory, charging the user, and scheduling the delivery operations into a single service. We can then handle everything using transactions within the same service call. However, this design forces us to share databases across services, breaking a microservice best practice.

- **Design 2:** We implement our inventory check as `reserveABook(..)` and `returnABook(..)` functions, which scan for availability and increase or reduce the book count. We can use a transaction manager to perform distributed transactions for payment.

- **Design 3:** We implement the flow using workflows, with or without transactions. In the latter case, we use compensation support, which is built into the workflows.

- **Design 4:** We can choose to first ship the book and then deduct the money, and in the case where the logic fails, we can take the hit and not charge the customer. Alternatively, we can get visual check and manually charge the customer.

- **Design 5:** We can implement the system as a simple sequence without recovery and write a task that visits the database, finding any buy orders that are not processed and what state they are in, and then recover the processing.

Transaction processing is slow and often a bottleneck. Yet, as the design options show, imaginative designers have many choices at their disposal.

Leadership Considerations

Making decisions about storage and consistency can be one of the trickiest tasks for architects.

Two frequent missteps are going beyond transactions even when it's unnecessary and building a system that assumes transaction guarantees when they're not needed.

We are typically caught between two considerations:

- Solutions that are more complex than transactions are often significantly costlier (e.g., 10X) than simple database-based systems.

- Modifying the data model later is often expensive because it often leaks into the user experience. This issue can't be resolved even with a system rewrite, because changing the APIs or user experience isn't always feasible.

Therefore, there's no single recipe for success here. It demands judgment.

Even when an ACID database can meet our needs, we should take care not to expose ACID guarantees to the end user through our APIs or UIs, because it's difficult to modify these later.

Let's revisit the five questions and seven principles.

Question 1: When is the best time to market?

Question 2: What is the skill level of the team?

Question 3: What is our system's performance sensitivity?

Question 4: When can we rewrite the system?

Question 5: What are the hard problems?

If system performance is a critical factor, the data model often poses a tough problem. You'd need to carry out a proof of concept and verify that the proposed data model can meet performance requirements. Management needs to establish minimal processes to ensure that performance standards are upheld. Furthermore, going beyond transactions demands high skill levels from the team.

Principle 1: Drive everything from the user's journey.

Principle 2: Use an iterative thin slice strategy.

Principle 3: On each iteration, add the most value for the least effort to support more users.

Principle 4: Make decisions and absorb the risks.

Principle 5: Design deeply things that are hard to change but implement them slowly.

Principle 6: Eliminate the unknowns and learn from the evidence by working on hard problems early and in parallel.

Principle 7: Understand the trade-offs between cohesion and flexibility in the software architecture.

Often, we can start with a simple single transaction-based system with APIs that expose only minimum guarantees and reassess our design when we redesign the system. If we thoughtlessly apply a microservices architecture, we might end up having to execute distributed transactions across databases, which we should strive to avoid. A simple single transaction-based system, even if it goes against microservices best practices, is often the quickest and easiest to implement. For more details, refer to Chapter 10.

When we're dealing with clouds, issues related to maintaining consistent data can become more pronounced because of increased delays. These scenarios need to be thoroughly tested.

In some situations, like in banking, maintaining both large-scale and strong data consistency is crucial. Making transactions work in these scenarios requires specialized knowledge and particular hardware and software solutions. For instance, properly configured Oracle systems on specialized hardware can deliver high performance but come with a substantial price tag.

It's rare that you'll need to go beyond ACID databases. When in doubt, choose ACID databases. You may need to make the decision and shoulder the risks.

Summary

Following are key takeaways from this chapter:

- When handling failures, transactions reduce the complexity and simplify the code we must write as we develop the system.

- We often use transactions with databases, but other sources such as JMS brokers, services, and workflows may also support transactions.

- If the transaction includes multiple transaction sources, we call it a distributed transaction and implement it with a transaction manager.

- Transactions are slow, yet distributed transactions are even slower, but we can avoid distributed transactions.

- Most systems have a database as the single transaction source, which needs a transaction manager.

- In advanced scenarios that require performance and scale, we can avoid transactions by redefining the problem to require fewer guarantees or by using compensation. The resulting systems are complicated, and we should use these techniques only when necessary.

8

Macro Architecture: Handling Security

Security involves securing the system's points that communicate with the outside, managing users, and making sure only authorized users can perform actions on systems, data, and any assets belonging to the organization. Security also involves ensuring that the data and the systems are handled according to the rules and regulations enforced by law or voluntarily by the organization, while balancing costs and risks.

Security is a broad and specialized area. To fully understand the role of security in your overall architecture and the trade-offs involved, you often need to seek the help of a security architect. The following discussion has two goals. The first is to help you understand how security fits into your overall architecture and its trade-offs. The second is to help you understand when you should enlist a security expert.

We can implement most security aspects either from scratch or by using middleware or cloud services. I do not recommend implementing security constructs from scratch, unlike other parts of the design, unless under extraordinary circumstances. Why?

- Security is risky, and there is little room for mistakes. Implementing your own security system is asking for trouble unless there are extraordinary circumstances, such as your system needs a very small memory footprint (e.g., less than 10MB).

- A simple use case needs to handle password management, password recovery, multifactor authentication, anomalous logging detection, and so on, creating a series of never-ending new feature requests.

- It is best to outsource these requirements to a middleware or cloud service provider. There's a lot to handle here, and if you choose to start from scratch, you will end up investing significant effort and time and still not get it right.

- Security is standards-driven (e.g., OpenID Connect and OAuth), making it easy to adopt tools for implementation. At the same time, not implementing specifications properly when executing your systems hinders your ability to integrate and work with other systems. Getting specifications correct often requires a lot of work.

- There are relatively cheaper cloud security solutions.

- When a user logs in at the start of a session, the user information can be remembered for hours. Because authentication happens once for the session, network latency induced by the cloud provider is often manageable if carefully implemented.

Using security tools is also a continuum. For example, we can choose to connect to open-source libraries and build the solution we need, which imposes the most cost and effort. Alternatively, we can use a cloud service that gives us greater flexibility. In this chapter, we discuss these security topics:

- User management

- Interaction security (including authorization)

- Storage, GDPR, and other regulations

- Security strategy and advice

User Management

User management handles identities and authentications. First is creating, storing, and managing identities and associated credentials, where authentication verifies the request to ensure the claimed identity sends it. Let's explore the typical use cases a system requires when managing users.

We often start handling identities as simple configurations; the Tomcat user file (tomcat-users. xml) is one good example. More advanced implementations use databases or LDAP (Lightweight Directory Access Protocol) such as Active Directory to store identities. Systems also can use identity and access management (IAM) products. Identities, credentials, and associated data represent a significant risk to the organization, where any compromise can be costly both in terms of money and reputation.

Moreover, having multiple identities for the same user often leads to confusion, mistakes, and poor UX, while increasing risks. The security architecture should, therefore, avoid duplicating identities, either through all systems referring to a single LDAP/identity server or through identity federation.

In addition to these caveats, user management and authentication require many features. For example,

- User registration and onboarding: This includes setting up profiles and credentials and inviting new users or guests into the system. Doing so sometimes also includes supporting custom workflows such as manager approval.

- User authentication methods: This includes passwords, tokens shared through emails and token generators, SMS, letters, mobile apps, and biometrics such as fingerprints and voice recognition. A specific deployment can use one or more of these methods or can apply them based on trust levels.

- User logins: Using their account with their own identity enables reusing identities from large internet service providers like Google and Facebook. This is a win-win situation because users do not need to remember new account details, and the system does not need to store and handle credentials.

- User federation: Organizations often let users from other organizations log in using their own credentials, which is called *federation*. Many organizations have different systems and will let the users log in once and then use any of their systems without logging in again. This is called *single sign-on (SSO)*.

- Contingency features: Users may also require profile updates, password recovery, and other contingencies arising from the use case.

The security system has a full view of when users log in and, often, what they do. This is the best place to build a user profile with user activities, which can be useful for marketing, sales, and customer support. For example, the user profile includes

- Audit logs and support investigations

- User credentials, including SSH keys, passwords, and other authentication methods

User management is also evolving with concepts such as decentralized identities, which might become a requirement for future use cases. In mid-size and large organizations, which include many integrated systems working together, onboarding and managing the employee lifecycle can be complicated. This effort may include provisioning accounts and managing processes related to the accounts across the different systems. Based on the system you are building and the size of your organization, you may require a different subset of features. Clearly, they are too complicated to build from scratch (unless you are building a security product).

The next dimension to understand is that not all users are created equal. Organizations usually handle four types of users:

- Public users who visit the website and products anonymously

- Registered users or customers who use the organization's services

- Internal users or employees

- Superusers and privileged users

Each use case focuses on a subset of users, where feature requirements vary significantly based on the user category. For example, when users are customers, the focus is on scale and ease of use, and when users are employees, the use cases may require complex authorization models, audits, and permission management.

Initially, the market for user management was called IAM (identity and access management). However, the required scope for all IAM features proved to be too broad, and in the last few years, different vendors have focused on different market subsets, thus breaking the IAM market into three parts:

- CIAM (customer IAM) focuses on customers.

- IAM focuses on employees.

- PAM (privileged access management) focuses on system administrators.

In the new model, however, products from each market have a lot more depth. This depth makes the architect's job much more complicated because the security solution requires integration of multiple products. If your system is simple and requires only user management, you can directly connect to LDAP (e.g., Active Directory) for users. If you require additional features, you may need to use an IAM product.

Interaction Security

The first steps with security are to get the basics right. This means setting up certificates and reminders to renew them and then using SSL for interaction between customers to your systems, whether that's a website running in the browser or a mobile app. All programming languages we use have support for SSL when connecting to other systems, and we should use those languages.

While considering user authentication, some interactions have multiple registered users and some don't. For example, our bookstore users create an account and then use the bookstore. These are interactions with users. Conversely, we can use many mobile apps and web pages without creating an account. These are interactions without multiple registered users. It is worth noting that applications for one registered user behave similarly to those with no registered users.

In this chapter, we call applications and scenarios that have multiple registered users *multi-user applications*, and the others we call *non-multi-user applications*. Examples of non-multi-user applications are anonymous mobile applications such as weather applications or where the system's client is another system. When we handle non-multi-user applications, we have several choices:

- We can use an API management solution. API management enables us to expose a service securely to users outside our team. After exposing an API as a service, we get an API key that our clients can use to securely do API calls using SSL.

- We can use mutual SSL. The SSL client also provides an SSL certificate and then connects only if its certificate is trusted.

- We can use cloud providers. These providers also provide a special type of account called a service account, which is intended for automation-related tasks, such as Google service accounts (see https://cloud.google.com/iam/docs/understanding-service-accounts).

Considering multi-user applications and related interactions, Figure 8.1 shows the different security roles involved. These roles can live in a single application or can be scattered across multiple services. Understanding this setup makes our discussion much easier.

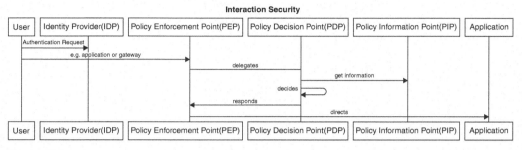

Figure 8.1
Security roles for multi-user interactions.

The identity provider (IDP) offers user management and authentication. When users call the application, the policy enforcement point (PEP) intercepts the call and invokes the policy decision point (PDP) to make an authorization decision. The separation of PEP and PDP allows for a specialized authorization logic evaluation. PDP often needs more information, which it might get by calling the policy information point (PIP). Sometimes, the IDP plays the role of PIP. Other times, authenticated tokens issued by the IDP include all required information, and PIP is not required.

The next two sections discuss authentication and authorization techniques used with multi-user interactions. In our discussion, we often refer to roles described in Figure 8.1.

Authentication Techniques

Authentication applies only to multi-user interactions. The simplest option is to use HTTP Basic Auth, where the application asks the browser to prompt for the user name and password and sends a representation with the request. Once the user is authenticated, the system remembers the authentication session, and any other requests in the same session are allowed without a challenge. Instead of a password prompt, most systems now use an embedded HTTP form or forward the user to a dedicated authentication form from the initial (home) page. The rest of the authentication flow works as before.

The recommended authentication flow never sends passwords to the server. Rather, clients demonstrate they have the password or the security key (e.g., using a shared key or public-private key pair) by encrypting a random challenge string sent by the server and then sending it back. If the server can decrypt the encrypted challenge and reproduce it, the server knows that client has the correct key.

Even with this architecture, many attacks such as SQL injection and *cross-site request forgery (CSRF)* can happen, but we do not discuss these attacks here because to do so is outside the scope of this chapter. (If you need more information about these attacks, many websites can provide details.)

With older architectures, services are authenticated by calling the database, LDAP, or identity server when a request is received. In such cases, they play the role of the IDP. The state-of-the-art solution is to use an identity server and a token-based approach such as OAuth as described in Sam Newman's book, *Building Microservices* (O'Reilly Media, 2015). Figure 8.2 depicts this approach.

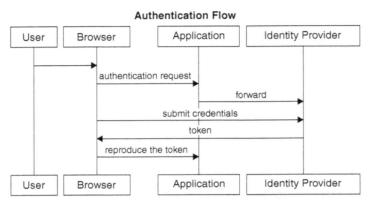

Figure 8.2
A token-based approach to authentication.

With the token-based approach, when clients come to our website or mobile app, we direct them to an IDP. The client sends their credentials to the IDP, which authenticates them. Then they receive a signed token with SAML or OpenIDConnect that describes their roles, and the information comes back to our application. Our system verifies the token and authorizes the calls based on the user roles described in the token.

This model pushes the authorization to the application. For example, with this model and the same request, a user with the role *publisher* might see different results than a user with the role *admin* because they have different permissions. Most IAM providers support this architecture. We expand this topic in the next section.

Note that the client can get the token and reuse it throughout the session. Hence, authentication needs to happen only once per session; therefore, the overhead of the additional call to authenticate is small. This approach enables us to use cloud-based IAM solutions widely.

Authorization Techniques

Authorization applies only when the interaction includes users. For authorization to work, the system administrators need to explain to the system when users are allowed and what actions they can carry out. For example, system administrators can ask the system to allow users in the admin group the right to delete users. As such, authorization requires several decisions:

- How to express authorization logic?

- Where to place the logic?

Let's explore authorization logic. Authorization logic needs to support two kinds of queries. The first query is given a user, a resource, an action, and whether the user can perform an action on the resource. The second query is given a user, all the resources they can use, and the actions they can carry out. The latter query is required for building reasonable user experiences because showing a user some resources and then denying access to the same resource leads to unpleasant user experiences. If you're interested, see Sam Scott's article "Why Authorization Is Hard," which provides a detailed discussion of this topic.[1]

We can always use code to express whatever logic we want. However, this approach forces developers to change code to modify authorizations. Furthermore, it also forces developers to reinvent the authorization model every time a change is needed. Supporting the what-are-my-resources query with this approach takes painstaking work, and keeping it in sync is not easy either.

The next level of authorization includes access control lists (ACLs), which are usually stored in a database. The database records identify who can do what operation(s) in the system. Fortunately, ACLs can support the what-are-my-resources query. However, specifying individual user permissions is tedious and hard to manage if there are lots of users.

The most widely used authorization model is called a role-based access control (RBAC). This model includes users, groups, permissions, and roles. As Figure 8.3 shows, a group is a collection of users. Permissions are things users can do within the system, and roles are a collection of permissions. Authorizations are defined only as the mapping between groups and roles.

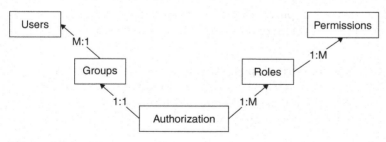

Figure 8.3
A role-based access control (RBAC) authorization model.

Say that, in our bookstore example, we want to let the bookstore admins add or remove items in the shop. To support this use case, we define a bookstore admin role and then list the

---

1. https://www.osohq.com/post/why-authorization-is-hard

resources and the actions allowed by that role. Next, we define an admin user group and give permission for users in that group to perform the admin actions for the bookstore.

Unlike ACLs, RBACs do not require that we add a rule for each new user added. Typically, the IDP holds users and groups, and the application or authorization part of the system holds permissions, roles, and mappings between groups and roles.

RBACs can support what-are-my-resources queries as well. Most identity and access management systems— IAM, CIAM, and PAM (see the earlier "User Management" section for clarification)— support RBAC, and most systems can work with a simple authorization model on top of users, groups, roles, and permissions. For example, Azure's model has consumers, contributors, and admins as default groups. Additionally, we can use the same model or extend or create a new model as needed. My recommendation is to use the same model when possible.

RBAC also has its limitations. For example, there is no simple way to tell if the owner of each item can edit or delete the item (such as a book in the bookstore).

An extended form of RBAC, which supports advanced queries, is called Relationship-based access control (ReBAC).[2] Google's Zanzibar is a comprehensive authorization model built using these ideas, and you can find an open-source implementation of it at https://github.com/ory/keto.

ReBAC is not yet widely supported by most IAM providers. My recommendation is that RBAC is sufficient for most use cases, but more complex authorization models are possible. Let's look at two in the following section.

Complex Authorizations Models

Let's look first at attribute-based authorization, where authorization is defined as rules based on the user's attributes. For example, a bank's rule may say that a user can create a regular account only if the user is older than 18 years. Often, an IDP provides tokens that assert the attributes, and the applications use the tokens to authorize. How to support a what-are-my-resources query is not clear in this instance.

Furthermore, it is possible to use a fully token-based approach, where we issue users tokens explaining what they can do, and the users send them back when they want to interact with the system. The primary advantage of this model is that it's decentralized; tokens issued by trusted IDPs can give rise to a rich security landscape. However, a token-based approach poses several challenges.

In this approach, the user needs to store and manage those tokens, which is harder from the user's perspective. The user might inadvertently (or maliciously) give those tokens to outsiders. Revoking permissions is also complicated. Finally, supporting a what-are-my-resources query is difficult.

---

2. https://en.wikipedia.org/wiki/Relationship-based_access_control

These complex authorization models are implemented using XACML (Extensible Access Control Markup Language) or Open Policy Agent (OPA), but you should seek help from a security architect if adapting these models. Next, let's focus on where to place the authorization logic.

Coupling Authentication and Authorization?

We can combine authorization (PEP, PDP, and PIP) with authentication and put that into an application or keep it separate. Although there can be exceptions, coupling authentication and authorization is often a bad idea because the associated code for each is written by different developers at different stages of development.

Considering each role, PEP is either an application itself or some code such as a gateway or an HTTP filter fronting the application. PEP extracts necessary information and calls the PDP. The PDP is your authorization model. For example, if you use the Kito Zanzibar implementation, that is your PDP. Alternatively, you can have your PDP implemented as a custom service. My recommendation is to keep PDP separate.

If tokens include all the information, PIP is not required. Otherwise, a database or an IAM server might play that role. In the next section, we discuss how we can implement common security interaction by combining these ideas.

Common Interaction Security Scenarios for an App

When we build an application, security scenarios are driven by two primary considerations: is the client code running in a trusted environment, and does the application or system include users? An example of a trusted environment is an API call done from a secure system, whereas an untrusted environment is a mobile app or web page, where the end user can look at the application and extract the embedded credentials. This leads to the following scenarios, presented as four cases.

Table 8.1 compares the trusted and untrusted environments with multi-users and non-multi-user applications. Each cell in the table discusses techniques that we can use in that particular situation. For example, for the multi-user's case, where the client is in an untrusted environment, we can use backend-for-frontend (BFF)–based architecture. BFF is often called a backend for the frontend or secure backend.

Table 8.1   Security Scenarios for Your App for Different Situations

	Non-Multi-User Applications	Multi-User Applications
Client in a trusted environment	Case 1: API keys, SSL mutual authentication, or service accounts	Case 2: API keys, SSL mutual authentication, or user tokens
Client in an untrusted environment	Case 3: Users are anonymous	Case 4: User tokens with or without BFF

Case 1: A Trusted System Making API Calls with Non-Multi-User Applications

An example of this use case is calling the OpenAI API from an application running in our data center. When the client is trusted, and there's no risk for the credentials to be compromised, we can use following approaches:

- API keys with SSL (Typically, users get API keys by logging in to a web page; e.g., developer portals for API managers or for Google, Amazon, and so forth.)
- Mutual SSL
- A service account if the API supports it

Case 2: A Trusted System Making API Calls with Multi-User Applications

An example of this case is a server-side web application (e.g., JSP or PHP-based) that makes calls to an API. There are several ways we can implement this case:

- We can use API keys with SSL and determine the user from the API keys.
- We can use mutual SSL and determine the user from SSL certificates.
- We can use SSL and send a user token issued by the IAM system with the request.

Case 3: An Untrusted System with Multi-User Applications

Single-page (web) applications (SPA) and mobile applications that support end users creating accounts and logins fall under this category. With untrusted clients, any credentials we put into the client can be extracted by the user and used for attacks.

For example, let's assume we are writing a mobile app for the bookstore. Users of the mobile app can extract any API key or credential we put into the mobile app. Hence, we have to either authenticate the users with something they already know or put credentials outside of the mobile app. We can do the former without a BFF by passing a user token. We can do the latter using a BFF, where the users make API calls. Let's look at each choice.

Choice 1: With a Secure Backend (a.k.a. Backend for Frontend, or BFF)

There are two ways to get a secure backend. The first is to create an API (BFF) for that purpose only, which can be used with mobile or web apps. The second is to use server-side technology (e.g., JSP, PHP) to generate the website and then use the server side as the BFF. Note that this approach works only with web apps, however.

Figure 8.4 depicts how security is handled with a BFF. In the figure, we pass Bob's token to the BFF and verify the validity of the token to authenticate users. To call the API from the BFF, we can either use API keys, Bob's token, or an exchanged token, based on what is required by the backend APIs.

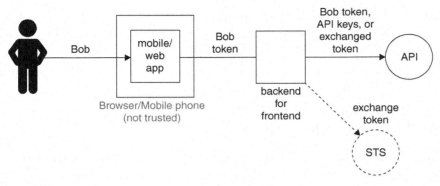

Figure 8.4
Security setup with a BFF (a backend for the frontend or a secure backend).

It is important to understand the concept of secure token service (STS). Our application talks to some APIs that may not understand tokens issued by our IAM system. In such cases, we talk to an STS, which accepts tokens issued by IAM and gives us a token accepted by the target API.

For example, if our API talks to the Google Map API, it likely will not accept tokens issued by our IAM. Instead, STS issues a token that Google understands. Architecturally, STS keeps token-issuing code in one place and avoids scattering it across many parts of the system. Most IAM vendors support an STS. However, setting this up and configuring it requires a security architect.

Choice 2: Without a Secure Backend (a.k.a. Backend for Frontend, or BFF)

Applications can work without a secure backend, but this is possible only if the APIs used by the application support and are aware of the users. Figure 8.5 shows the application prompting users to log in. After they've logged in, they need to include the user token with the backend API, which happens via SSL/TLS. This approach is possible only if the backend API supports the same users and groups as the frontend.

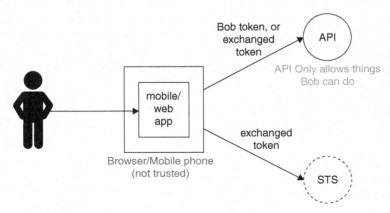

Figure 8.5
Security setup without a BFF.

If the backend API does not support the same users, the application should use an STS to exchange the user token for a token supported by the backend as described in "Choice 1: With a Secure Backend." This complex case requires help from a security architect.

In both of these choices, an STS or a backend API should check authorization. The recommended approach is to use a separate PDP as Figure 8.1 shows.

Case 4: An Untrusted System with Non-Multi-User Applications

An example of this case is a mobile app that does not have a registered user (consider a weather mobile app). In this case, we do not have a user registered in our system to send a token as in case 3. Because the client (the mobile app) is not trusted, we can't give any credentials to it. Hence, our users are anonymous. We can't provide any permissions-based checks, and we need to handle unfair use by some form of user throttling.

Storage, GDPR, and Other Regulations

Data stored on disk for a long time poses many challenges to the organization. Because a disk holds "concentrated" data a long time, the risks associated with that data are much higher. Let's look at some examples.

Stored data is often the target of many attacks, which can damage the reputation of the organization for losing its data this way. When the compromised data includes confidential user profiles or credit cards, for example, the harm can be massive, in addition to a direct loss of money.

A significant risk vector is your employees, who can misuse or inadvertently share sensitive data outside the workplace. Your ability to audit and control the data used by employees is complicated. Also, leaks can happen through the organizational partners, who may have relaxed security guidelines or have intentionally misused the data (e.g., Facebook and Cambridge Analytica).

Many organizations serve a wider global audience. US, Europe, and several other countries now have regulations for customer data that is stored for a long time. It's likely that more countries will adopt similar regulations. It is, therefore, a good practice to design your system for regulations like GDPR even if you are not covered by those regulations currently. Regulations such as GDPR (General Data Protection Regulation) and PSD2 (the revised Payment Services Directive) assert that holding such data comes with implied obligations. For example,

- GDPR mandates organizations to secure users' personally identifiable information (PII), such as Social Security numbers, mailing or email addresses, and phone numbers, and to delete it on request.

- PSD2 obligates banks to expose their data as APIs.

- US healthcare regulations compel organizations to share their data via APIs.

Furthermore, the right for information laws, as well as law enforcement agencies, might require organizations to share their data. Additionally, if you support users from multiple jurisdictions, you may have to hold the data in the corresponding jurisdictions to protect the rights of each group of individuals.

From a security point of view, it is best to hold as little data as possible. However, data can be a source of a significant competitive advantage, which creates an interesting dilemma. Moreover, it is not simple to pick and choose what data to keep because it is often not easy to guess which data would be valuable five to ten years from now and which data isn't. Following are some of the best practices for handling data.

First, decide which data carries high risks. Doing so requires a detailed audit of types and brainstorming their use. Second, separate sensitive data and securely store it in an encrypted manner (for example, replacing PIIs with UUIDs). Most analytics and machine learning use cases do not require knowing exactly who the user is, and this allows us to store data as UUIDs, thus avoiding the need for keeping PIIs. This approach enables us to delete PII data, and the system will still continue to work, considering the user as an anonymous user. Furthermore, separating PIIs from other sensitive data allows us to respond to GDPR queries easily.

The best practice is to store all sensitive data as UUIDs (for example, system or activity logs, audits, or transactions) and keep PIIs only in your IAM system. This approach limits PII storage to IAM, which you can guard with many layers of security. Sometimes, it is possible to convert a PII to a non-PII. For example, we can remove the last few bits of an IP address or store the country or organization of the IP address instead.

If PIIs are required and need to be retained, we should keep them in a separate storage area and encrypt them to guard against leakage, even if someone hacks into the databases holding them. It is a good practice never to hold decryption keys in plain-text files. Instead, issue a service call to get the decryption password.

Another risk is that a search can leak data, even if no PIIs are returned. Circumstantial evidence might be enough to identify an individual user, violating their privacy. For example, if there is only one person older than 70 in a certain area, a search on anonymized medical reports might let someone guess the owner of some reports. Regulations like HIPAA (The Health Insurance Portability and Accountability Act) cover this topic.

Third, define who has access to data and why and then set up processes that govern access and audit the processes. As discussed, any access to PIIs should be carefully guarded. Another best practice is to keep the data in the cloud or a data center, letting users remotely work on the data (for example, using Python Jupyter [iPython] notebooks), while making it hard for them to take data out of the system. This approach can help a lot in reducing mistakes as well as planned attacks.

Sometimes, organizations want to share or integrate data with partners. As happened with the much discussed Cambridge Analytica case, partners may have lax security requirements or might even misuse the data (as happened in the aforementioned case). When an organization gives a partner or a tool access to its data, it has to ensure that those entities can also maintain the same level of security precautions. Instead of sharing data outright with partners or tools, in some cases, we can expose an API that shares the data in a controlled manner.

Unfortunately, other than APIs and a few experimental techniques that we discuss shortly, technology does not help solve the data-sharing problem. Often this problem is handled through legal agreements and processes.

The recommendations mentioned in this section are not exhaustive. Some regulations are domain-specific (e.g., HIPAA for health data). You should talk to a security consultant who is well versed in your domain to identify all the requirements and can handle them accordingly.

Security Strategy and Advice

This section presents a few strategic considerations for security architecture. As we discussed, because the margin of error for security design is narrow, starting with a naive or simple design and gradually improving it is not recommended. Instead, my recommendation is to adopt an IAM or CIAM product and build the architecture on top of those products.

The ability to analyze data and extract insights is a major competitive advantage. Therefore, organizations should enable their employees to run experiments as needed and without too much red tape. If trying out an idea requires a lot of paperwork and weeks of waiting, chances are a lot of good ideas will not get tried at all. We need to hit a balance between security risks and the cost of adding friction through processes. This is the responsibility of the technology leader.

IAM or CIAM systems can be hard to replace, although not impossible, so you must consider your current and future requirements carefully before choosing a system. In your design, as much as possible, keep the option open for switching to a different IAM or CIAM if required, unless doing that incurs significant costs.

Most tools use monthly active users (MAUs) as a pricing yardstick, and it is a good idea to seriously consider your current and future MAU needs before making the final decision on which system to choose. This argument also applies to storage. Available tools support GDPR; however, most tools provide little or no support for sharing data with partners, forcing us to build that part ourselves if needed.

When designing the architecture, we should keep authorization logic separate and simple, but we also need to consider potential future complex authorization requirements as part of the design. My recommendation is to choose an RBAC model or a ReBAC model. Having said that, let's look at a few other considerations for IAM architectures.

Performance and Latency

With a current de facto security design, which forwards the user to another system to be authenticated, performance could be a challenge. The user would first authenticate to get a token, which they will then use to invoke the system again and again. We call those system invocations the *system access path*. We need to carefully watch the latency of this path because that part is triggered often, and it significantly affects the UX. We can optimize this path by reducing database calls to check permissions (for example, by keeping the permission model in memory or by exclusively using tokens) and by reducing the need for complex cryptographic operations such as public-key cryptography.

Token checks also need to scale with the rest of the system. If those checks are stateless (make the decision only by looking at the request when tokens are used), it greatly simplifies the scaling design. In addition, latency challenges often surface, not as average latency spikes, but as tail latency spikes, where the latter is much harder to debug because they are harder to recreate. Tail latencies often occur in cache-miss paths, so careful and focused testing at development can save a lot of time later.

Zero-Trust Approach

Historically, we defend systems by securing the perimeter and trusting users within the perimeter. However, attacks have significantly increased by multiple factors as IoT, mobile phones, and APIs are becoming more common. Organizations may also have to integrate with other systems and partners, which also complicates the attack surface, and it increases the risk of parameter breaches. It is worth noting that these engagements and integrations add significant value to the organization, and staying disconnected is often not an option. It is the architectural leader's responsibility to communicate the importance of these integrations.

To handle elevated risk, security experts have stressed the need to switch to a zero-trust model, where we secure each service independently by authenticating and checking permissions for all calls in the system. This approach moves us away from a perimeter-based model. With the zero-trust model, there is no perimeter where we trust the users inside. Instead, users are authenticated, authorized, and continuously validated at each step of the way.

In contrast to the old model, where we authenticate and check permission at the edge, the new model requires us to use code to check permissions and authorization at each service. Consequently, security appears in more places in the system, and the performance of the security becomes even more critical.

A key principle in zero trust is to limit the blast radius. One way of doing this is to use the security principle of providing minimal privilege to the user. The second is to identify multiple levels of logins, where critical operations require higher levels of authentication (for example, more factors). To reduce the blast radius, we may need to require consent from multiple users before allowing extraordinary actions, such as downloading all users.

We often couple an anomaly detection system with zero trust, where the system detects any anomalies and either forces users to give additional authentication (for example, a new factor or questions based on previous user interactions) or forces them to re-authenticate. When we're implementing zero trust, it is worth considering the NIST 800-207 standard when applicable.[3]

Take Caution When Running User-Provided Code

Say our system executes user-provided code in some way that requires careful attention. This could be running user-provided JavaScript, Python, SQL, or Lua scripts or code, or adding user-provided parameters to an existing script. When a user uses the power of a script in input, it opens up many attacking possibilities. When this happens with SQL, it is called *SQL injection*, and careful use of libraries can handle most SQL injection cases.

Other scripts need careful auditing and testing. Even when we are running the user code as containers, the code has access to the internal network, which is a security threat. Also, all credentials provided to containers can be accessed via code running inside, which could let an attacker sneak into the system. One option is to use sandboxing technology such as gVisor (https://gvisor.dev/), Firecracker (https://firecracker-microvm.github.io/), or Kata Containers (https://katacontainers.io/).

Blockchain Topics

Another topic that warrants our attention is blockchain. Using blockchain for a decentralized identity and for audits that can't be tempered with are key use cases for this approach. The essential advantage it provides is that users, claims, or records are taken out of the control of an individual organization, increasing the organization's trustworthiness. A company that is often mistrusted (e.g. organic food provider) can use such technology to create verifiable and auditable records, thus creating significant competitive advantages.

Despite the promise, wide attention, and concentrated efforts from Hyperledger (https://www.hyperledger.org/) and Ethereum (https://ethereum.org/en/), blockchain has received only limited adoption, likely due to technical challenges and associated complexity. However, the potential is real, and it will likely be more fully utilized in the future. We should keep our eyes open to the benefit from any future developments.

Other Topics

Another challenging topic is denial-of-service (DoS) attacks, which are designed to render a service inaccessible. Using firewalls can solve DoS problems to some extent, but it is difficult if not impossible to completely fend off a carefully focused DoS attack. When we're handling

---

3. https://csrc.nist.gov/publications/detail/sp/800-207/final

this type of attack, running in the cloud might be the best option because we can use our cloud provider's default protection and firewalls. Another new idea being considered is pushing the authentication to the edge, stopping distributed denial-of-service (DDoS) attacks at that level. DDoS attacks are used to overwhelm a targeted website with fake traffic.

Even if we have a lot of experience, a lot of risks are associated with security. It is the unknown that gets us into trouble, and the more eyes reviewing the design the better. I recommend a detailed audit with an external expert. Also, it is important to foster a culture where any potential risk can be brought up and examined. It is the leader's responsibility to get a balance between risk and speed of change, without which the organization will die slowly or very fast.

It is not enough to just secure the system. With new regulations and the potential for users to sue, it is important that security be handled with as much professionalism and visibility as possible. If a breach happens, it is important to be able to show that all practical precautions were made. Certification from external parties can provide this visibility.

Leadership Considerations

Finally, let's reconsider the five questions and seven principles described in Chapter 2. Here are the questions and the principles again as a reminder:

Question 1: When is the best time to market?

Question 2: What is the skill level of the team?

Question 3: What is our system's performance sensitivity?

Question 4: When can we rewrite the system?

Question 5: What are the hard problems?

Principle 1: Drive everything from the user's journey.

Principle 2: Use an iterative thin slice strategy.

Principle 3: On each iteration, add the most value for the least effort to support more users.

Principle 4: Make decisions and absorb the risks.

Principle 5: Design deeply things that are hard to change but implement them slowly.

Principle 6: Eliminate the unknowns and learn from the evidence by working on hard problems early and in parallel.

Principle 7: Understand the trade-offs between cohesion and flexibility in the software architecture.

Considering questions 1 and 4 and principles 2, 3, and 5, we can use different security features when they are not required for our current use cases. It's important, however, that whichever feature we release, it must have deep security. As discussed earlier, we can't start designing security with the simple solution and build up from there. For example, we can't implement authentication with an old but simple algorithm or architecture and improve it later because it might have vulnerabilities.

Another related aspect is that we do not want to lower the security design, unlike other designs, to suit the team's skill. We need to have the required minimum skills in the team or hire an expert as a consultant and use that expert to enhance the security skill levels of the team over time.

Considering questions 2 and 5 and principle 6, a common challenge with security is latency. It is important to consider latency in the design and carefully measure it in the system, adding instrumentation to monitor it. Most security capacity problems (e.g., database overload) surface as latency problems, and it is paramount that we have enough instrumentation to support the isolation of problems. Also, new architectures often employ multiple HTTP forwards, which also creates latency and can lead to timeouts.

Considering our hard problems, securing against different attack patterns is difficult, and as mentioned, we need the help of an experienced professional to get this right. Taking any kind of user input and running user-provided scripts are often weak points, which enable attacks (for example, SQL injection, cross-site scripting [XSS]).

Furthermore, security can easily interfere with our UX design. For example, a complicated password policy may stop many users from signing up. It is up to the security designer to think from a user's point of view and to make the user's experience as painless as possible. For example, if the user's password does not match our policy, the system should tell which part of the policy is not correct rather than providing a blanket message. Adding things like email verification can also reduce conversion, delaying the user or detaching them from their first user experience. It is the technical leader's responsibility to find the balance between security and UX.

Considering principle 4, security itself is a trade-off. The most secure system is one in which you do not give access to anyone, but such a system is not useful. It is the responsibility of the architect to find the right balance in this trade-off, as discussed previously. Sometimes the leaders need to take the responsibility (and risk) to enable designers to make progress with the program.

In summary, handling security in a macro architecture is a complicated topic and deviates from other topics we discussed. The main idea is that it may be OK to delay the additional security features, but whichever feature you choose to support requires a deep security design. It is best to adopt a CIAM or IAM solution and build on top of that, but you must get it right the first time and enlist external expertise if you must.

Summary

Security is a key consideration in any design. Following are key takeaways:

- Security is complex. My recommendation is to implement security on top of IAM and other products or SaaS services, rather than implementing those use cases ourselves.

- We can use LDAP for simple cases, but we require an IAM product for complex cases.

- Security use cases can be categorized as multi-user or non-multi-user applications. We handle non-multi-user applications using an API solution, mutual SSL, or service accounts.

- Security in multi-user applications can be complex. We can handle them with authentication and authorization, or we can combine them with trusted and untrusted clients.

- Due to associated risks, we can't first implement a simple version and improve later with security use cases. Similarly, we can't simplify a security design to suit the team's skills.

- Problems in security architecture often manifest as latency problems.

- Data stored on disk poses many risks to the organization. At the same time, this can provide significant competitive advantages. Leaders need to balance the potential gains and associated risks.

- Data handling is regulated by various countries, and it is wise to either support these regulations in our designs or to leave open the possibility of complying with them in the future.

- Running user-provided code can introduce complex vulnerabilities.

9

Macro Architecture: Handling High Availability and Scale

This chapter discusses how to add high availability (HA) to the system design and scale the system as needed. Because HA keeps the system available despite failures, let's look there first.

Adding High Availability

With high availability, the system is available round the clock, without interruption. It is widely accepted that if a user reaches out for a system and it is not available, the user may foster a negative impression, which leads to the loss of that customer. Although for decades, it was normal for businesses to be open only during in-office hours, now everyone accepts that fact that internet apps are available 24/7, so you need HA. There are two primary approaches for HA: replication and fast recovery. The following sections discuss each approach.

Replication

Replication (see Figure 9.1) means to have backup copies (replicas) in the system such that the copy can take the place of the original if it is unavailable. Either all replicas can actively serve traffic, or one replica can be on standby. We call the former case an active-active setup and the latter an active-passive setup. As we discuss later (in the "Understanding Scalability" section), the challenge is to keep copies in sync and up to date.

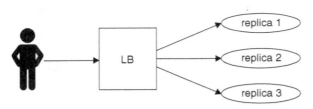

Figure 9.1
Replication.

Because most architectures come down to stateless servers and databases, replication also involves syncing databases. Most databases support this kind of data sync as a feature. You can configure the database so that changes to one get replicated to another. Some databases support an active-active replication, whereas others support only the active-passive setup. If you are just looking for HA, often an active-active setup is too complicated, so I recommend going with an active-passive setup.

To get the HA setup right, we must handle several problems. First, how would the customer know the address of the server and replica? Often, we use a load balancer in front of the services to route traffic. For this, we can utilize software load balancers, such as nginx, TCPProxy, or Apache mod_proxy, or we can employ hardware load balancers such as F5.

Next, what if the load balancer fails? There are several ways to handle this situation:

- Use a DNS configuration.

- Hot-swap the IP.

- Use a keepalive package.

- Implement load balancers for your hardware.

First, we can use DNS configurations to remove failed nodes from the DNS list. However, this failover takes time (due to caching), and users would see the failures. Second, if you have access to advanced network routers, they can hot-swap the same IP to a new node, which is the most elegant way of handling failures. Cloud platforms handle this as a feature.

If you plan to run on-premise, you can also achieve HA by using the keepalive package for Linux.[1] This package uses the Virtual Redundancy Routing Protocol (VRRP). Finally, hardware load balancers have built-in redundancy and can recover failures. In my opinion, hardware load balancers are the most reliable, and IP hot-swap is next. If neither one is available, my recommendation is to go for the keepalive package.

To scale up, systems create a hierarchy of such load balancers, combining several types. For example, the hierarchy will often have hardware load balancers or DNS load balancers at the top and use software load balancers as branch nodes in the hierarchy.

---

1. See https://tldp.org/HOWTO/TCP-Keepalive-HOWTO/usingkeepalive.html

There are two wide approaches to arranging replicas: first, replicating each component of the system, and second, replicating the system as a single unit (e.g., having two parallel systems). Figure 9.2 shows the two approaches. Both approaches work. For clarity, I do not show interactions between components.

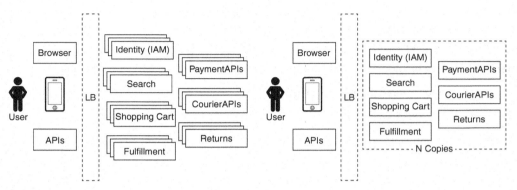

Figure 9.2
Replica arrangement options, where we can either copy each system component or duplicate the entire system.

We can implement the first option shown on the left side of Figure 9.2 using load balancers. We discuss how to implement the second option, shown on the right side of Figure 9.2, in the next section when discussing the shared-nothing architecture. Also, because the second option lets us keep two independent systems, it is simpler in design, thus more stable, easy to manage, and less prone to mistakes.

When we set up load balancers, if the system has a session state that lives only in the server memory, the user will face difficulties. For example, when the server sends a second request, the load balancer can send it to a new server, and the user's session is no longer available.

We can handle this scenario by using sticky sessions, where the load balancer always sends the requests from the same user to the same server. Even with sticky sessions, if the server fails, the session is lost, and users will have to log in again. However, this is a rare occurrence, and many designs accept this approach.

An alternative is putting the session state either in the user's browser or in a database where each node can handle the second request. If the data is in the user browser, we will have to add session data to every request. If we put data in to the database, we will end up doing more database calls, which adds latency and often reduces throughput.

Fast Recovery

Two downsides of replication are that it consumes more resources, and failure paths are not tested often. Alternatively, if we can recover quickly, the effect of downtime is minimal. With fault tolerance, we can improve availability, given mean time to failure (MTTF) and mean time to recovery (MTTR), then

$$Availability = MTTF / (MTTF + MTTR)$$

Using replication increases MTTF, which increases availability. Alternatively, if we can reduce MTTR, that also improves availability. This idea was first conceived by the concept of recovery-oriented computing (ROC), and this is the second approach to achieving HA.[2]

A system can achieve recovery through several means. When a failure occurs, the system can

- Shut down and restart on fresh resources
- Isolate the affected area and restart that part of the system, or micro-rebooting[3]
- Use a self-healing algorithm that detects and reassigns its tasks when a node has failed[4]

With any of these approaches, as with replication, the system needs to recover its state. For example, both new and old systems can share the database, whereas databases in both systems can use replication to recover from database failures while the rest of the system uses fast recovery.

This idea works closely with GitOps, where we keep all the system information including configurations in a code repository, and we can boot the system from that location without any manual intervention. This approach enables us to create a new copy of the system when needed. Given the availability of cloud and on-demand computing resources, this is a viable approach.

While the system is recovering, it will be unavailable for a small period of time. The user application can show a message to the user and retry automatically, given that the system can come back up quickly.

Fast recovery is cheaper, more flexible than replication, and easier to scale. It is much more stable with most failures. However, fast recovery requires three preconditions:

- All components and services must restart within 2–3 seconds. Cloud, containers, and Kubernetes make it possible to restart a computer quickly, and our design needs to optimize the services running on the machine so they also start fast. One approach is lazy loading, where services start and load data from data structures on demand or in the background.

---

2. See https://en.wikipedia.org/wiki/Recovery-oriented_computing

3. See "Microreboot—A Technique for Cheap Recovery," by George Candea, Shinichi Kawamoto, Yuichi Fujiki, Greg Friedman, and Armando Fox, at https://www.usenix.org/legacy/event/osdi04/tech/full_papers/candea/candea.pdf

4. See "Self-Stabilization" by Marco Schneider at https://dl.acm.org/doi/10.1145/151254.151256 and "Self-Stabilizing Systems in Spite of Distributed Control" by Edsger W. Dijkstra at https://dl.acm.org/doi/pdf/10.1145/361179.361202

- Services or components need to be able to start concurrently without a specific order. Otherwise, it takes too long to bring up the system.

- The new system needs to get an up-to-date state from the old system. One common approach is replicating the database but quickly recovering the rest of the system.

However, despite the advantages, to fully adopt fast recovery, you need to automate the recovery process. Kubernetes (https://kubernetes.io/) handles this situation to a greater extent through its fault-tolerance features. Kubernetes error recovery, however, is not error-proof. For example, if the node CPU is high, Kubernetes restarts the node, which can lead to a restart loop unless we handle the failure. We need to consider potential error conditions carefully and then handle them appropriately.

Understanding Scalability

We define *scalability* as the ability of a system to handle higher throughput with more resources while keeping latency within acceptable bounds. In my opinion, the term *scalability* is misleading. It seems to suggest that the system should scale indefinitely. No system scales forever. As per our earlier discussions on design, I think the right question is how much load we will need to handle before we must rewrite the system.

Often, scaling is not required. For example, using default architectural choices, we can design an HA-based, nonscalable system that provides a throughput of 50 TPS (transactions per second). That is 129 million requests per month. Even assuming 10 times peak load, our system in this case can handle 10 million requests per month, which is enough for most real-world situations.

In terms of design, we often either overdesign or underdesign for performance. Few understand scalability, and many systems do not account for that. The few who do understand scalability often overdo it. They want to design systems that are worthy of Google load but, in the process, make the design complicated and fragile, which often leads to failures and delays. The article "You Are Not Google" by Oz Nova details how rarely a typical system would face the same scaling challenges as Google, but a form of *scale envy* (as in math or physics envy) tempts us to design systems that scale more than needed.[5]

The designs of systems that handle hundreds, thousands, or even hundreds of thousands of requests per second are drastically different and require different levels of effort, expertise, and hardware. It is a mistake to design for 10,000 TPS when you need only 1,000 TPS. It is worth noting that traffic usually correlates with your organization's income, and therefore, when there is a huge increase in traffic, you will have the money to rewrite the system.

We scale by running on larger nodes or running on many nodes. We discuss the first approach in Chapter 10. To understand scalability, it is useful to understand the Universal

---

5. See https://blog.bradfieldcs.com/you-are-not-google-84912cf44afb

Scalability Law (USL). Let's look at one equation for this. Although it looks a bit scary, I promise you: The bottom line is simple.

Given an app running with p nodes, *scalability* is the throughput ratio between the system with p nodes versus the system with a single node. Throughput ratio is given as follows:

$$C(p) = \frac{p}{1 + \sigma(p-1) + \kappa p(p-1)}$$

This equation has three parameters:

- The number of nodes (p)
- Contention (σ), which is the cost of synchronizing multiple execution threads that can run on many machines
- Coherency (k), which is the cost of keeping the variables in different nodes in sync

Let's consider the ideal case, which is zero contention and zero coherence cost; in that case, scalability with p nodes will be p. We call such an architecture a *shared-nothing architecture*.

Coordination between nodes and any data that is kept synced brings down the performance quickly. For example, using 0.1 for both contention and coherence, scalability with ten nodes is 0.9, which means a ten-node system runs slower than the single-node system. Indeed, as discussed in the paper "Scalability! But at What COST?" by Frank McSherry, Michael Isard, and Derek G. Murray, many complex systems underperform a competent single-node implementation.[6] Architects who design distributed systems without a careful understanding of performance often create a slower system despite enormous effort and complexity.

Now we can get to the bottom line of our equation: Scaling is about keeping coordination and data sharing to a minimum. To scale, we need to reduce data sharing and coordination.

Scaling for a Modern Architecture: Base Solution

Before scaling, you need to understand the limits of a single node and your performance goals. At a minimum, you need to do a PoC to understand the single-node performance. Sometimes, it is possible to tweak the single node to achieve your performance goals. If so, you should use that option because it will save you a lot of complexity in development and operation.

A modern architecture almost always includes many stateless services and a database. We can scale such a system by running multiple copies of our services, and because they may be stateless, replicas will not need to talk to each other. Then, all coherence and contention overhead happen in the database, and you will be limited by your database. You can reduce the overhead on the database by caching data. Also, you can push any work that happens in the background to a queue and process that using a batch system and different computers.

---

6. See https://www.usenix.org/system/files/conference/hotos15/hotos15-paper-mcsherry.pdf

If you are limited by the database, you can scale the database. Modern database systems can scale a lot, although doing that typically requires special hardware and heavy subscription fees.

This architecture works for many systems, but there are more sophisticated ways of scaling your system. The rest of the chapter discusses the details. However, for most systems, the base solution is enough. My recommendation is to go to the advanced techniques only in the second and third iterations of your system.

Scaling: The Tools of Trade

The default scale design creates *N* replicas and runs them side by side in active-active mode. However, as the USL suggests, this design works only if replicas do *not* communicate. If they do communicate a lot, coherence and contention overhead take over, and the system will not scale.

In Chapter 6, we discussed how to build systems by first identifying the building blocks that we can use, then implementing any missing logic as services, and finally, using a coordinating layer to connect everything together. Different building blocks have different scaling characteristics.

The following architectural concepts severely limit scale if they are in the critical path because they involve communicating between multiple nodes:

- Distributed coordination including distributed locks and synchronization between threads (barriers, signaling, and so on)
- Shared variables
- Replication or ordered-reliable multicast
- Transaction managers

We can still use these elements in our scalable design, but they can't be in the critical path affecting every request or most of the requests the system processes. On one hand, they might be OK in a limited way (for example, for leader elections at the initialization of the system). On the other hand, when we design scalable architectures, the following building blocks are scalable:

- Load balancer
- MapReduce systems
- Enterprise service bus (ESB)
- Container/VM management
- Distributed hash table (DHT)
- Gossip architectures
- Tree of responsibility

Further, the following can be made to scale moderately (five to ten nodes) by careful design. However, most production-grade implementations are not scalable out of the box:

- IAM server
- Databases
- Message broker
- Workflow
- API manager
- Registries
- Distributed cache

Our goals for scale should affect our choice of the building blocks. For example, when we choose a database, that choice often impacts the scale. Often, a back-of-the-envelope level estimation of the limits of the building block can save us lots of trouble later.

If we consider other parts of the system, most services are scalable if we can scale the underlying databases. Then, we connect services and building blocks using the coordination layer. When we implement the coordination layer, there are four tactics (techniques) to keep communication low, and they help us scale. Let's look at each.

Scale Tactic 1: Share Nothing

This first idea is simple in concept: Break the system into N similar parts that do not share anything, and then you can scale by using the load balancer to route traffic among the parts. Using this approach is sometimes simple, but at other times, it's complicated or impossible. If possible, this is the preferred approach due to its simplicity and ability to deliver maximum scale.

Scale Tactic 2: Distribution

With this second tactic, we can break the problem into N partitions and assign each partition to different nodes. For example, a bank may separate customers into partitions and route traffic for different customers into the corresponding partition. The challenge is to partition the system such that the communication between partitions is minimal. Furthermore, when a node fails, we need to recover part of the problem (e.g., customers in the bank case) and assign them to a new node.

Scale Tactic 3: Caching

When the bottleneck is data retrieval, with this third tactic, we cache frequently used data. This approach reduces the effective reads seen by the data source. For example, when the database is a system's bottleneck, we can increase the scalability by caching the reads for 1 second, thus reducing the traffic received by the database by this client to 1 TPS.

Scale Tactic 4: Async Processing

If data processing can be done in a less restrictive timeline, it increases the load the system can handle. For example, some banks consolidate the transactions at night as a batch process, increasing scalability. Similarly, if the data can be prefetched, that avoids database access, which increases scalability. When we implement asynchronous processing, the queues are a useful tool that we can use to absorb short-term spikes. However, if the system behind the queue can't handle the long-term average message rate, the queue overflows.

In the next section, we further discuss how to use these tactics to scale a system.

Building Scalable Systems

When we build the first version of our system, as we discussed, if it meets our scalability goals, we are done. Most systems would have a database setup with an active-passive configuration, multiple stateless services talking to the database, and a load balancer to route the required traffic services. We may also use one or more building blocks (see the earlier section "Scaling: The Tools of Trade"). Figure 9.3 shows the bookstore as a sample system to scale. (We use this as a running example throughout the remainder of this chapter.) For clarity, I do not show interactions between components.

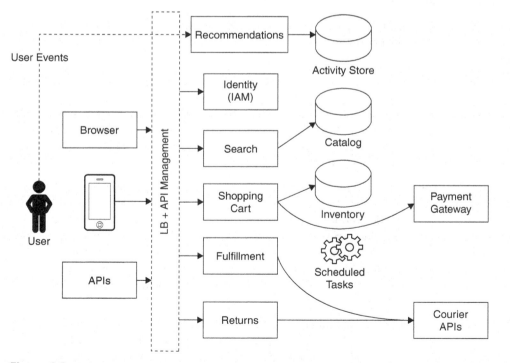

Figure 9.3
A sample architecture for a bookstore.

If we fall short of our scaling goals, there are two broad approaches to scaling a system. First, find bottlenecks and improve that part of the system. Second, use a shared-nothing architecture by building a self-contained unit that you can scale.

Approach 1: Successive Bottleneck Elimination

As mentioned, the first approach when scaling is to find where the bottlenecks are in the system. We can often find this either by understanding the system (a fingertip feel for the performance, for instance) or by collecting data through observability. When we identify the bottleneck, we can verify that by bypassing the bottleneck (replacing it with a service that responds with mock results, for example) and checking the scalability limits without the bottleneck.

To scale further, we must find and improve the offending part of the architecture to reduce communications from that point. For example, we might find that our IAM system is the bottleneck. We need to either use a more scalable IAM system or change its design to be scalable (e.g., by adding more nodes).

One common approach is to give more resources to the system. We can do this by running the offending part of the system in a bigger machine (horizontal scalability) or by running multiple copies of the system fronted by load-balancing techniques (vertical scalability). Performance tuning and architectural improvements can also improve the scalability limits; however, the solution depends on the type of the bottleneck.

Once we have improved the bottleneck, if we are lucky, we will reach our scale capacity. If necessary, we need to find the next bottleneck and fix it too. We must repeat this process until we reach our goal.

Let's look at our bookshop example. Lots of users come and search for books, but only a small fraction buy. Therefore, we think the search and resulting recommendations are the likely bottlenecks. Because the book catalog is read-only, we can precompute recommendations. Hence, we can scale by creating copies of the search and the recommendation parts of the system. Further, because some items are browsed more often than others, we can cache these recommendations. Applying this approach will likely let us scale further.

If either the IAM server or the shopping cart becomes the bottleneck, we should improve these features. We can scale the IAM server by partitioning the users across many IAM servers and routing authentication and authorization requests to the corresponding authentication server (scale tactic 2). We can also scale the shopping cart by partitioning it by users and then partitioning the inventory by item ID (scale tactic 2). Because services are stateless, this process involves partitioning the databases across multiple nodes. This is called *database sharding*. When a single user buys items that belong to multiple item partitions, this means doing transactions across multiple shards using one of the techniques discussed in Chapter 5.

Also due to stateless services, scaling often comes down to sharding (partitioning the database) across multiple nodes or using a NoSQL-style database. Both require us to find a dimension (column) in the data that we can use to separate data into partitions, such that we do not have to issue a join via SQL for the data in different partitions to answer the queries. Several databases support sharding, but setting up and running a sharded database is complex and requires skilled professionals. Even with such skills, with some queries that need data from multiple shards, a sharded multiple-node database is slower than a single-node database.

After pushing through the bottlenecks in the IAM service and the shopping cart, the payment APIs may become the bottleneck. We will likely have to work with our payment API providers to scale this API.

As we saw in this example, we must find the bottlenecks in the system and then successively remove them until we achieve the scaling limits or we run out of ideas. When we do this, we should design with known scalable architecture building blocks and avoid those that do not scale.

Approach 2: Shared-Nothing Design

Another broad approach to scaling a system is the shared-nothing design. The idea is to run multiple copies in the full system while limiting the required communication between different copies. Figure 9.4 shows a bookstore design that applies this design. For clarity, I do not show interactions between components.

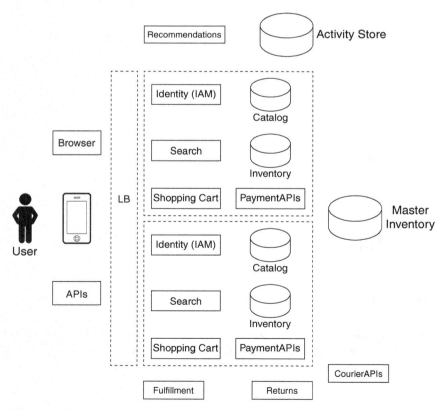

Figure 9.4
The bookstore's shared-nothing design.

As Figure 9.4 shows, we can run many copies of the system, each handling a specific partition of users (e.g., all users whose name hashes to a certain value). Everything else works the same, except the inventory. To handle inventory, we need to keep a primary inventory database, and each partition's inventory gets a block of items from the primary inventory, thus serving the users from the block of items (using a cache with reservation). If a partition inventory is out of items, it gets a new block, and if the primary inventory is out of items, it gets a block from other partitions (we call this *work stealing*).

For each use case, we need to figure out how to partition the data. For this use case, the idea of primary and partition inventories works. Different scenarios would need different ideas. For example, Figure 9.5 shows the architecture implemented to handle bank transactions. Keep in mind that this example is just for illustration purposes. The actual architecture of a bank is significantly more complex and takes into account many other factors.

With this architecture, we partition the work by users. Each user goes to only one partition. However, this approach can go wrong with transactions that involve two users who are placed in two partitions. Banks often update the balance at the end of the day, so we collect transactions and asynchronously reconcile them at that time.

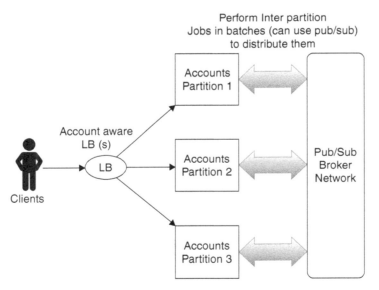

Figure 9.5
A design for handling bank transactions.

As we saw, we need different solutions for different problems, and some problems can't be scaled. This is what makes scaling difficult. If you are building a highly scalable system, seek to hire a team of five to ten developers who have experience with such systems.

Leadership Considerations

Both scalability and high availability are guided by nonfunctional needs, which are influenced by the business context. For instance, a system related to financial services often has rigid HA and latency demands. It's crucial to consider the entire business context when designing for HA and scalability.

High availability is fairly easy to implement once you grasp the technical details. But when things get complicated, it usually turns into a scalability problem.

A typical mistake that experienced architects make is overengineering for high scalability when it's not actually needed. A system that can handle tens of thousands of transactions per second is often much more complex (like ten times more) than a system that can manage hundreds to a few thousand transactions. Building beyond the necessary limit is wasteful.

Let's see how the leadership questions and principles apply in this case:

> Question 1: When is the best time to market?
>
> Question 2: What is the skill level of the team?
>
> Question 3: What is our system's performance sensitivity?
>
> Question 4: When can we rewrite the system?

It's usually helpful to figure out what's needed (question 1, question 2, question 3) and plan your design based on that. Most scalability issues can be fixed with a system rewrite. Despite common belief, it often takes longer than expected for high scalability to be required. And when it is, you'll have the resources to rewrite the system.

However, a system rewrite can take between six months and a year. It's important to keep an eye on trends and act proactively. But you shouldn't act without solid forecasts.

> Principle 4: Make decisions and absorb the risks.
>
> Principle 5: Design deeply things that are hard to change but implement them slowly.
>
> Principle 6: Eliminate the unknowns and learn from the evidence by working on hard problems early and in parallel.

If you decide that scalability is necessary, it becomes a tough problem. You need to approach it carefully by doing PoCs, careful tests, and reviews to make sure the design can meet the scalability targets.

Sometimes, you might need to decide not to design for scalability and bear the potential risks.

Summary

Following are key takeaways from this chapter:

- Most production systems need some kind of a high availability solution.

- Two broad approaches for HA are replication and fast recovery. The first approach avoids downtime but needs more resources than the second.

- With replication, when two copies actively serve traffic, we call this an active-active setup, and when one copy is on standby, we call this an active-passive setup.

- A system with an active-passive database setup and multiple services talking to the database with default architecture choices can handle 95% of the use cases.

- Different architectural building blocks have different scale characteristics. If you use building blocks with limited scale in critical paths, they will limit the scale of the system.

- Look out for Google envy. Scale systems only to the limits you need in the foreseeable future.

- When you must scale beyond your current design, you do so by successively eliminating bottlenecks or by using a shared-nothing design.

10

Macro Architecture: Microservices Considerations

Microservices are the new architectural style for building systems using simple, lightweight, loosely coupled services that we can develop and release independently of each other. Given the broad recognition of microservices, no architecture discussion is complete without a description of how microservices affect the design. In this short chapter, we discuss practical challenges when using microservices and potential solutions.

If you are new to microservices, I recommend reading Martin Fowler's post[1] for a definition. If you want to compare it with service-oriented architecture (SOA), watch Don Ferguson's talk "Some Essentials for Modern Solution Development".[2] Also, to help you decide

- When microservices are useful, see Martin Fowler's "Microservice Trade-Offs".[3]

- If microservices are worth doing, see Martin Fowler's "Microservice Premium".[4]

What problems do microservices solve? When we build a system with a team, we need to break the system into small parts that can be developed independently. If their parts depend on one another, the members of the team need to talk to each other. However, when the team grows beyond four to nine people, it becomes harder both for the members to

---

1. http://martinfowler.com/articles/microservices.html

2. https://www.youtube.com/watch?v=W7tGlxJtofI

3. http://martinfowler.com/articles/microservice-trade-offs.html

4. http://martinfowler.com/bliki/MicroservicePremium.html

communicate effectively and the leader to productively manage the team. Keith McEvoy's article, "What's the Ideal Team Size for High Performance," describes this phenomenon.[5]

To compensate, we break the team into multiple teams. However, communication across teams then becomes slower due to several reasons:

- Different teams have different priorities.

- Different teams understand the system differently, and they understand each other's parts differently.

- Different teams measure output differently.

- Trust across the teams is often less than trust within the teams.

Hence, need for even a small amount of communication across teams can significantly reduce the development velocity of the system. The primary goal of microservices is to break the system into small parts, which then can be given to different teams to reduce the need for communication between teams. We achieve this goal by making each microservice loosely coupled with others and assigning each microservice to one team only.

Simple, lightweight, loosely coupled services that can be developed and released independently of each other are indeed a worthy goal. If we can achieve this goal, we can reduce maintenance costs, and the system will evolve significantly faster than older-style systems (monoliths). Yet, there are many ways things can go wrong.

Building proper microservices-based systems is far from trivial. The following sections discuss how to handle some of those challenges. (Note that I use the abbreviation *MSA* in the rest of the discussion to mean microservices architecture.) Should you decide to go with MSAs, there are four decisions you must make. For each, we discuss possibilities and make recommendations.

Decision 1: Handling Shared Database(s)

Each microservice should have its own database, and two microservices *must* not share data via the same database. This rule removes a common cause that leads to tight coupling between services. As Figure 10.1 illustrates, if two services share the same database, the second service breaks if the first service changes the database schema. In this case, the teams will have to talk to each other before changing databases, which creates coupling and leads to delays. I think this rule is a good one and should not be broken.

---

5. See https://www.linkedin.com/pulse/whats-ideal-team-size-high-performance-mcevoy-business-accelerator/

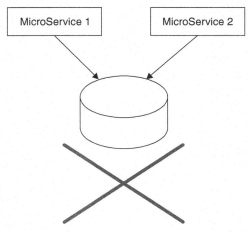

Figure 10.1
MSAs sharing the same database, which leads to coupling and delays when one microservice changes the database schema.

There is a problem with this rule. We often share the database when two services (e.g., bank accounts, shopping carts) use the same data and need to update the data transactionally using database transactions to enforce consistency, as we discussed in Chapter 7. Any other solution than sharing a database is complex. Let's explore a few.

Solution 1: One Microservice Updating the Database

If updates to the database happen only in one microservice (e.g., a loan approval process that needs to check the balance), you can use asynchronous messaging (message queue). This approach, shown in Figure 10.2, lets you share the data without sharing a database.

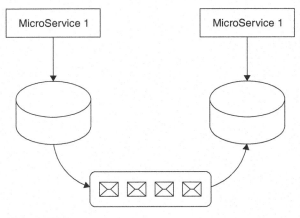

Figure 10.2
Using a message queue for updates to the database.

Solution 2: Two Microservices Updating the Database

If updates to the database happen in both services, either consider merging the two services or use transactions. The post "Microservices: It's Not (Only) the Size That Matters, It's (Also) How You Use Them" describes the first option: merging the services.[6] We already discussed transactions in detail in Chapter 7. Also, as we discussed in that chapter, sometimes it is possible to accept lesser guarantees such as eventual consistency, thus giving up the need for transactions.

When making a decision as to whether to share databases, we need to evaluate the complexity of defining the microservice scope to all operations that require the shared database and assigning it to one team versus the cost of using multiple microservices and handling communications between them.

Decision 2: Securing Microservices

The state-of-the-art solution is to use an identity server and a token-based approach such as OAuth, as discussed in Chapter 8 and shown in Figure 8.2. Sam Newman's book, *Building Microservices* (O'Reilly Media, 2015), discusses this solution in detail.

With the token-based approach, when clients come to our website or mobile app, we direct them to an IDP. The clients log in via IDP and receive a signed token with SAML or OpenIDConnect that describes their roles, and the application uses those tokens to authenticate and authorize the users.

Decision 3: Coordinating Microservices

When the program receives a request, the system talks to the microservices and then serves the request. We already detailed how to handle the coordination between different services in Chapter 6, and that discussion applies here.

Decision 4: Avoiding Dependency Hell

A key goal of an MSA is to make it possible for services to be released and deployed independently. However, that is possible only if service dependencies do not break amid changes to evolving service APIs. To do that, you must avoid "dependency hell." Let us understand the scenarios.

---

6. See https://cramonblog.wordpress.com/2014/02/25/micro-services-its-not-only-the-size-that-matters-its-also-how-you-use-them-part-1/

Let's first consider microservice A supporting the API A.v1, then upgraded to API A.v2. Now there are two cases: one for backward compatibility and the other for forward compatibility.

Backward Compatibility

In this case, microservice B might be already using A.v1 and sending messages intended for A.v1 to A.v2. Supporting this is known as *backward compatibility*. There are two ways to handle this situation.

The first approach is to keep backward compatibility for the API so that A.v1 messages do not fail with the A.v2 endpoint. For example, we can add optional parameters but can't remove or rename existing parameters. As much as possible, we need to use this approach because it incurs the least complexity.

When it is not possible to keep the API-level backward compatibility, we must run both A.v1 and A.v2 services and route requests to the right version of the API using a load balancer. However, both A.v1 and A.v2 must share the same persistent data model (e.g., database). If our services are stateless, sharing a data model often happens without additional work by the developer.

The compatibility support should be bounded by time to avoid complications. For example, you may have a rule that no microservice should depend on an API that's older than three months (pick a suitable time period here). This rule would let the microservice developers eventually drop some of the code paths supporting the older versions. Supporting backward compatibility is a necessary condition to receive the benefits of the MSA.

Forward Compatibility

Consider microservice C, which is using A.v2. If, at some point, A.v2 runs into an issue, and you need to revert the API back to A.v1, then microservice C must be able to send messages intended for A.v2 to A.v1. This is known as *forward compatibility*.

Handling this forward compatibility is complicated, however. If the A.v1-to-A.v2 change is not backward compatible, when we upgrade A.v1 to A.v2, we need to answer this question: If there is an issue with A.v2, what can we do? There are several choices:

- We can try to set up a fallback path that receives A.v2 messages and then calls A.v1.

- We can choose to create a fallback path later if needed.

- We can decide to give up riveting from v2 to v1 and handle any issue with other means (for example, restarting the system or finding a temporary fix until a proper fix is found).

If we use the first option, setting up a fallback path to receive A.v2 messages but then work with A.v1, any new feature in A.v2 will not work. If we use the second or third options, we should do our best to reduce the risk of a problem occurring. For example, we can take extra care in testing. Furthermore, we can initially enable only one dependent service to use A.v2 and test that with production before all dependent services switch to A.v2, thus reducing the blast radius.

Ultimately, forward compatibility is only a temporary measure, and we cannot rely on that for all services forever because services in use often acquire more dependents with time. It is much better to avoid the need for forward compatibility by preventing the need to revert to a newer version.

How to handle forward compatibility choices is about managing risk, and even with support for forward compatibility, significant risk of downtime remains. It is important to be objective about the risks. Leaders need to consider possibilities and make solid decisions. The posts "Taming Dependency Hell within Microservices" by Michael Bryzek (https://www.infoq.com/news/2015/06/taming-dependency-hell/) and "Ask HN: How do you version control your microservices?" (https://news.ycombinator.com/item?id=9705098) are good discussions about related topics.

Finally, it is better to avoid the problem altogether. Using Postel's law in design—*"be conservative in what you do, be liberal in what you accept from others"* (mentioned by Bryzek)—can improve chances of both forward and backward compatibility. Furthermore, a thoughtful and deep API design (Chapter 2, principle 5) can go a long way in reducing the need for API changes altogether.

Dependency Graphs

If we draw all our services in the system as nodes, and if we draw lines from A to B when A uses data from B (e.g., service calls and events), we get a dependency graph of the system. The shape of the dependency graph is a design choice.

One option is to freely invoke other microservices whenever it is needed. That creates a spaghetti architecture from the pre-ESB era. I am not a fan of that model. It can lead to deep invocation paths, creating complexity. Deep invocation paths can lead to timeouts, and they are hard to debug.

The other extreme is to say that microservices should not call other microservices, and all calls should be done via the coordination layer, leading to a one-level tree. For example, instead of microservice A calling microservice B, we bring the result from microservice A to the coordination logic, which calls B with the results. This is the orchestration model. Most of the business logic now lives in the coordination layer. Yes, indeed, this makes the coordination layer fat. Trying to achieve an absolute one-level dependency graph makes code complex because parameters need to be passed around. For example, if service A wants to use service B, now service A has to change the coordination layer.

Keeping dependency graphs two to three levels deep is a good idea, balancing both sides. My recommendation is to keep dependency graphs simple.

Loosely Coupled, Repository-Based Teams as an Alternative to Microservices

Most microservice success stories come from large companies (e.g., Netflix, AWS), where each microservice has enough work to tie up a two-pizza team (a team that can be fed with two pizzas). In practice, I often see services that are much simpler, which can be developed and managed by one full-time developer or even one part-time developer. Trying to achieve loose coupling between such fined-grained microservices often creates more complexity than it reduces. If we go back to the fundamentals, there is an alternative that reduces cost significantly.

As we discussed, with MSA, we want to make our teams independent from other teams. Teams need to be able to write code, release builds, and then take new versions to production without coordinating or waiting for other teams. The reason we want to remove the dependency between teams is that even a small amount of dependency results in a drastic reduction of the output. The books *The Phoenix Project* by Gene Kim, Kevin Behr, and George Spafford[7] and The Unicorn Project by Gene Kim[8] beautifully explain this issue with plenty of examples.

When we realize that our goal with microservices is to have multiple two-pizza teams and let them work without the need for coordination, we can achieve the same dependency with the following approach. I first saw this approach described in the book *Ask Your Developer* by Jeff Lawson.[9]

- The system is developed by two-pizza teams of programmers, where each team owns a repository.

- We apply microservices' principles as if the code in the repository is a microservice. The code can be one service or maybe several, based on its complexity. For example, it is OK for the code within the repository to share a database, but it is *not* OK for the code owned by two different teams to access the same database.

- When the team grows (say, for example, six to seven people where we are approaching a seven to nine team limit), we start the process of breaking the team into two. This includes splitting the repository into two parts and assigning one part to each of the two newly formed teams.

On one hand, the cost of communication between developers in the same two-pizza teams is small, so we do not need to expend a lot of effort to make the code within the team loosely coupled. On the other hand, we must keep the code across teams loosely coupled.

---

7. IT Revolution Press, 2013, https://itrevolution.com/product/the-phoenix-project/

8. IT Revolution Press, 2019, https://itrevolution.com/product/the-unicorn-project/

9. Harper Business, 2021, https://www.askyourdeveloper.com/

Even within the same repository, the team may choose to facilitate the eventual separation of code to the two repositories in their design when the cost is not prohibitive. The only disadvantage of this approach is the cost of splitting teams. However, any complex microservice over time needs to be split. Architects can make decisions anticipating the eventual split but should, as much as possible, avoid expensive commitments (not sharing the same database, for example). I believe this approach provides great balance between the advantages and costs of using an MSA.

Leadership Considerations

Two common errors with microservices involve using them with small teams and thoughtlessly implementing them, which leads to complex architectures.

Microservices let us split the structure into many loosely connected parts that can be developed, released, improved, and managed independently. The best way to dodge these issues is to keep the preceding goal in mind and think from first principles.

Considering the first, a single team should ideally consist of seven to nine people. If your team is smaller, microservices aren't necessary because they won't solve any existing problem.

Furthermore, microservices work well when all your services require a team of seven to nine people. But this isn't always the case. Some services need fewer people, whereas others need more. The idea of using repository-based teams allows a team to manage several services when services are fine-grained. If services are complex and need larger teams, we can split the service into two services and two repositories.

The suggestion to start with a monolith aligns with repository-based teams, where we split the service into parts only when the team grows beyond a two-pizza size.

Considering the second mistake, as much as you can, avoid a situation where two services (or two repositories in repository-based teams) are modifying the same data model. If these two teams share a database, they'll need to communicate their changes, slowing everyone down. Not sharing a database means each team needs to communicate through events or distributed transactions, adding a lot more complexity.

If you're using microservices, ensure each team deploys their code independently. Understand and resolve any challenges. Following microservices principles without independent deployment won't benefit you.

In this area, it's good to be skeptical. Think from first principles and ensure the recommendations actually help your team. What worked for Amazon and Netflix won't necessarily work for you.

Two common mistakes with microservices are applying microservices with small teams and blind application of microservices that leads to complex architectures.

The best way to avoid those pitfalls is to remember the goal.

Microservices allow us to break the architecture into several loosely coupled parts that can be developed, release, evolved, and managed independently.

Summary

Following are key takeaways from this chapter:

- When building a system with more than four to nine developers, we can use microservices concepts to create multiple two-pizza teams that can develop, release, and deploy their code to production with minimal need for coordination between teams. Such teams can provide a much higher rate of output compared to a system built as a monolith.

- Not sharing databases between microservices creates complexity. We should define the scope of an individual microservice, balancing the costs and gains of fine-grained microservices and the cost of syncing data across two databases.

- We must support backward compatibility in our microservices when APIs change. Handling forward compatibility, however, is complex, and we must make a judgment call based on the associated risks.

- When services are fine-grained, microservices can create more complexity, which offsets any gain. In such cases, we can assign a repository to each team and apply the microservice principles to a repository rather than to a service.

11

Server Architectures

In earlier chapters, we discussed architecture at the macro level. Service is the fundamental component of those designs, which implements functionality that we can't borrow among architectural building blocks. This chapter explores how we can implement well-designed, efficient, and stable services.

Writing a Service

Several frameworks (e.g., Spring Boot, Ballerina) let you write a service. In each case, you adopt a template that looks something like this:

```
Response do-something(request){
    //code
    response = ...
    return response
}
```

The request object represents the user's input, typically JSON, XML, or a binary protocol such as Protocol Buffers. We then process the request, carry out what is needed, construct the response using the same format as the request, and send it back. Next, we give the port number to the framework, start it, and we have a service. If someone wants to access the service, it is available in the http://*your-machine-ip:port* location. If you are a decent programmer, you will get this done in a few minutes to a few days, based on the complexity of the service.

It is useful to understand how our service works. A service, when started, creates a server socket with a given port (e.g., 8008) and waits for a client. When a client (e.g., a mobile app running on our customer's phone) opens a connection, the server socket creates a new socket and hands it over to the service implementation. The service implementation reads the headers (usually HTTP); reads the message; parses it as XML, JSON, or another format; and then calls our do-something method using a thread it picked up from a thread pool. When our method finishes, the server sends the response back to the client and returns the thread to the thread pool. More complex implementations are possible, and we talk about them later in the chapter.

To some extent, we are already done with our service. However, we need to discuss a lot of details under the hood. This chapter first describes some best practices for writing services (using the methods we discussed previously). Next, we dig into advanced techniques such as different server architectures and how to use them in practice. Finally, as you may have guessed by now, I tell you not to use them unless it is necessary.

Understanding Best Practices for Writing a Service

The following are some guidelines for writing efficient and simple services:

- Just as with the larger architecture, it's crucial to maintain a level of separation and flexibility (loose coupling) between the components within a service too. To achieve this goal, we need to implement well-known software development best practices, like SOLID principles, DRY (Don't Repeat Yourself), KISS (Keep It Simple, Stupid), YAGNI (You Aren't Gonna Need It), and others.

- Do not reinvent the wheel. Borrow libraries and frameworks instead of writing code from scratch when the benefits outweigh the costs. Libraries and frameworks are typically more stable, are tested, and provide a maintained implementation, which means you do less work. They reduce financial costs as well as indirect costs, which include added complexity, architecture pollution, uncertainty, and, sometimes, performance overhead.

- Handling state within a service is complex. Write stateless services when you can and keep as little state as possible if you must keep it in the service. One way of doing this is to ask clients to remember and send the state with each request (e.g., using cookies). Do not keep any state in memory that you can't recreate at restart. Among examples of states that you can recreate are caches, pools, and indexes.

- When writing the code for the service, block the service thread as little as possible. A blocked service call keeps a thread away from the CPU. Although we can compensate by having more threads, that also means higher context switch costs, as discussed in Chapter 3. For example, if you call one service and then call another while waiting for the first, the time taken for both calls to finish will be less than calling them one after the other. Unfortunately, nothing is free. Not blocking often requires asynchronous programming, which is complex and hard to debug.

- Use pools to reuse complex objects, such as clients that call services and database connections. Each pool has a queue. Monitor queue lengths and create back pressure if the queues are full. We discuss this topic more fully in Chapter 12. As discussed in Chapter 2, get a thin slice working as early as possible. Additionally, test the performance, profile the code, and iterate as you add more functionality. The most critical path in a service is serving the requests. The next critical path is server startup. Do as little as possible on the critical paths. For example, read configurations and deployments on startup or in the background. Always take your time to tune the critical path.

- Most services get the request, do a read or write on a database, do a few service calls, and do some processing and returns. Database calls and service calls take time, increasing the latency, so

    - Cache what you can.

    - Prefetch the values if possible (start an asynchronous call to fetch them as early as possible).

    - Batch the reads and writes if possible.

    - Take time to tune the database (e.g., slow query logs).

- If services call many other services or APIs, they will have high latency. You may have to use nonblocking calls so that the external service calls happen in parallel.

- Controlling both the client and server gives us better performance and reliability guarantees, such as message order. Also, keep in mind, in this case, you can easily change things in the future.

- Idempotent operations do not have any effect even if they receive multiple copies of the same request, so make service operations idempotent whenever possible. Then it is easy to recover, and you can live with at least one delivery. This makes your macro architecture simple. For example, as we discussed in Chapter 7, you can often avoid transactions if all your stateful services are idempotent.

Having followed these guidelines, if the service does what you want with the expected performance guarantees, then you are done. The rest of the chapter discusses more advanced service design techniques. However, my recommendation is to start with the default server architecture, unless the performance is critical for your use cases. If you are using advanced techniques, hire a few experienced developers who have implemented the same or similar techniques before.

Understanding Advanced Techniques

So far in this chapter, we have focused on the most straightforward server architecture, using blocking I/O to read and write data from the network and making use of a thread-per-request (thread mode), which we call *thread-per-request* architecture. With this design, service developers can write code as usual, blocking I/O and other blocking operations. This approach provides the simplest user programming and debugging experience. It is not the most performant architecture, but it provides acceptable performance in most use cases. Hence, the thread-per-request architecture is an excellent choice for most use cases.

In the rest of the chapter, we discuss advanced techniques. Although these techniques give developers more power, each also brings a bit of complexity. Use them with care and only when needed.

Using Alternative I/O and Thread Models

In advanced architectures, we vary the I/O and thread models from thread-per-request architecture. As discussed in Chapter 3, a system achieves the best performance when running with a thread count close to the number of CPU cores while keeping each thread busy doing useful things. We usually accomplish this with an event-driven thread model, which keeps context-switching costs to a minimum. However, if there are any task blocks (for I/O, for example) in this architecture, the CPU will idle waiting for blocked tasks, and the performance of the system will reduce significantly.

We must implement such architectures carefully. These observations suggest several conclusions:

- When using an event-driven thread model, we must use nonblocking I/O. Thus, the thread model and I/O model are interrelated.

- The service implementation must do all other operations in a nonblocking manner, passing the burden to the service programmer. This forces the programmer to learn new techniques.

- In some cases, blocking is unavoidable. In those cases, we need a hybrid model.

We already know the thread-per-request model and event-based model. One widely used hybrid model is called staged event-driven architecture (SEDA), a nonblocking I/O with processing arranged in a pipeline. Let's explore each model in detail.

Thread-per-Request Architecture (TRA)

With TRA architecture, a single thread does all the work for a single request. Figure 11.1 assumes each request has three work items. All work items in each request are assigned to one thread. If all the threads in the thread pools are exhausted, requests must wait.

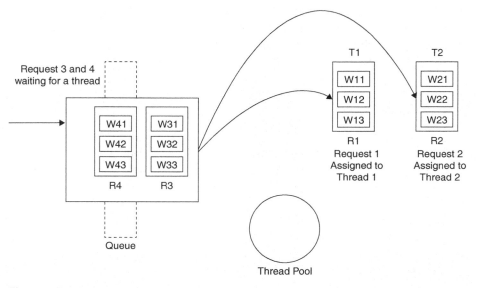

Figure 11.1
Thread-per-request architecture (TRA).

To understand this architecture, let's map it hypothetically to the real world. Imagine a restaurant that operates using a TRA, where a single person (a thread) does all the steps involved with ordering: seating the customer, taking the order, cooking, serving, giving and processing the check, and imparting the final greeting. That person remains idle in between customers (e.g., while patrons are eating), doing nothing worthwhile when "idling." This is a wasteful scenario because the restaurant needs the same number of wait staff as tables.[1]

As another example, consider a stock market service that receives a buy request, calls an API to get stock quotes, and buys the stock if the quotes are within the given price range. With this model, all processing happens in a single thread. Having sent an API call, the thread idles, waiting for the response. Even though both scenarios are not ideal, there are three main advantages of TRA:

- It provides the most natural programming model for service developers.

- Several frameworks (e.g., Spring Boot, Tomcat) already support this model.

- The implementation itself is easy to understand.

The main disadvantage of this model centers on the number of threads that we want to use for our service. We must carefully pick an appropriate number of threads. Once all the threads are exhausted, the system must wait for a thread to be free to accept new requests.

---

1. This example is influenced by the article "What Is SEDA?" at https://stackoverflow.com/questions/3570610/what-is-seda-staged-event-driven-architecture.

If we use a CPU workload for the service, the thread number should be close to the number of cores. If there is significant I/O, the thread number should be 50–100 times the number of cores to accommodate blocking. A higher number of threads increases the context-switching overhead, as discussed in Chapter 3. Consequently, this architecture is not the most performant in most use cases.

Event-Driven (Nonblocking) Architecture

Event-driven architecture requires that we break the processing into subitems that do *not* block. To achieve this effect, we often take work done between two blocking operations (e.g., I/O and acquiring locks) and assign them to one item. Figure 11.2 provides an example of this approach.

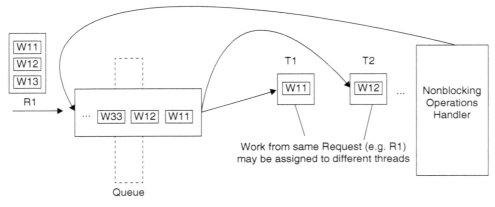

Figure 11.2
Event-driven (nonblocking) architecture.

To avoid blocking, we need to use a nonblocking API for blocking operations. Doing so breaks blocking operations into two parts: the beginning and the end. We begin by calling for the start of I/O and end the call when I/O is done. Often subitems start with the end part of a blocking operation and end with the beginning part. For instance, if we have a stock-buying service that calls two services for quotes, makes the decision, and sends a response, it can have three subitems, as depicted in Figure 11.3.

As Figure 11.3 shows, the nonblocking architecture sets up event listeners to receive external events (requests) and to schedule subitems in response to these events. The architecture may assign each subitem to a different thread when running.

For service calls, subitems must use nonblocking I/O operations. After the service call starts, the thread is released to take on new work. When the service call completes, the architecture schedules the next subitem with the service response and adds it to the queue. A thread picks up the subitem and processes it. This process continues until all subitems are done.

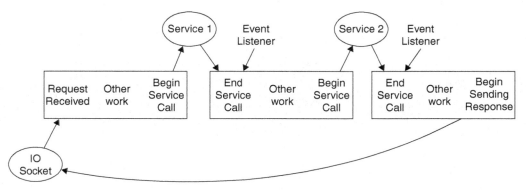

Figure 11.3
Example of subitems for a service doing two service calls.

If our hypothetical restaurant operated using event-driven architecture, every person (thread) needs to be able to do any task. They wait for an activity, and one jumps in and does the task (seating or ordering, for example). When the task ends, they go back and wait for a new task. This restaurant can work with much fewer wait staff than the number of tables; however, each person must be able to do all the tasks. Also, wait staff need not wait on a single table; rather, they need to submit work (an order) and then check for completion.

The key advantage of the nonblocking architecture is performance. The architecture operates with a fixed thread pool that's close to the number of cores in the system. Because none of the subitems get blocked, given there are enough subitems, this architecture can achieve close to 100% utilization. There are, however, two downsides:

- It is hard to make everything nonblocking.

- Writing nonblocking service implementations requires a deep understanding of how I/O works from service developers. Unfortunately, few developers understand I/O that deeply.

Staged Event-Driven Architecture (SEDA)

We use SEDA in response to the difficulty of making everything nonblocking. It brings the advantages of event-driven architecture without forcing us to make everything nonblocking.[2]

As Figure 11.4 illustrates, SEDA consists of multiple stages connected by queues. Each stage can use either a blocking or a nonblocking architecture. It often uses runtime tuning to find the best parameters (e.g., number of threads) for different stages. SEDA is conceptually similar to the manufacturing pipeline.

---

2. See "SEDA: An Architecture for Well-Conditioned, Scalable Internet Services" by Matt Welsh, David Culler, and Eric Brewer, in ACM SOSP 2001, available at https://dl.acm.org/doi/10.1145/502059.502057.

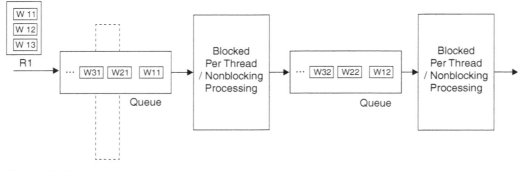

Figure 11.4
Staged event-driven architecture (SEDA).

Let's look again at our hypothetical restaurant. This time, it works using a SEDA-like architecture: different people (threads) process different stages. In some stages, one person may do all the processing, but in a different stage, multiple people might work together. This architecture allows for specializations (e.g., seating, cooking, serving, and so forth). And, if we go back to our stock-buying example, the stages would be processing the request, calling the API, making the decision, buying stocks, and sending the response.

The primary challenge for this architecture is that service developers need to identify the stages, which requires a deep understanding of the performance behaviors. Although many middleware frameworks use SEDA, it is not widely used by service developers to build day-to-day services due to the design complexity.

If we plan to use a SEDA-like architecture, we can build on top of a disruptor framework, which provides an efficient implementation of a staging architecture. As Figure 11.5 shows, the disruptor works through a circular buffer, and new work is added, moving counterclockwise around the buffer.

Processors belonging to multiple stages can simultaneously work with circular buffers, and we can control the order of processing by defining constraints. For example, a processor from the first stage (processors in Figure 11.5) can lock a cell, read, process, and write data back to the cell. The second stage processor also can read the cell, process, and write back to the cell. We can, however, define a constraint where processors from the second stage must never be allowed to access a cell before a processor from the first stage has written to the cell. This approach creates a SEDA-staged pipeline. Similarly, we can implement more complex stages including forks.

Disrupter frameworks reduce the memory cost of sharing data between threads through a careful data structure design that avoids cache invalidation. The disrupter adds additional savings in SEDA architecture by replacing multiple queues and data movements between them with a single circular buffer and constraints.

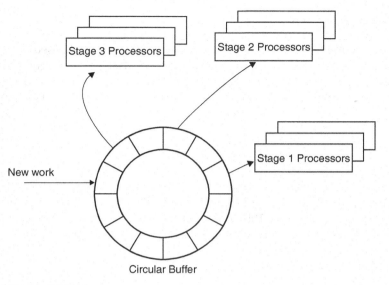

Figure 11.5
SEDA-like architecture on top of a disruptor framework.

Comparing the Architectures

Chapter 4.2 of Benjamin Erb's diploma thesis, "Concurrent Programming for Scalable Web Architectures" (https://berb.github.io/diploma-thesis/), discusses these architectures as well as some additional ones. In this chapter, I have excluded the multiprocessor architecture from my discussion because it is rarely used due to the availability of multicore architectures.

It is worth noting that, on one hand, implementing the nonblocking I/O with a thread-per-request architecture does not yield significant performance improvements. On the other hand, using a blocking I/O and event-driven model can lead to drastic performance penalties.

The three architectures described in this section provide a trade-off between the complexity of programming versus better performance. Because developer productivity is the critical goal, most service development and hosting frameworks use the thread-per-request model. You should also use the same through one of the frameworks such as Tomcat or Go kit. Only when extracting the maximum possible performance from the server is a crucial advantage should you choose to go with other architectures. In the following sections, we continue our discussion about advanced techniques.

Understanding Coordination Overhead

Performance behaviors can be counterintuitive. For example, sometimes a single thread-based implementation performs better than multiple threads, even in a multicore machine, due to coordination overhead. This happens because of Amdahl's law, which we discussed in Chapter 3. Two common forms of coordination overhead are I/O overhead and memory access overhead. Let's look at them next.

I/O Overhead

A single writer often performs better than multiple coordinating writers when writing to the same source. In such cases, it is better to submit data from multiple threads to a queue or LMAX Disruptor ring buffer and write the data using a single writer. This design also lets us buffer the data, reducing the number of writes required and improving the performance. This is called the Single Writer Principle.[3]

Memory Access Overhead

A single thread can outperform multiple threads even without I/O. This is especially true when computations scatter memory access or multiple threads frequently update one or a few variables.[4] In such cases, we should rewrite the code to use a single thread or optimize data exchange between threads.

At the OS level, each thread has its own cache and a programming counter. To prevent threads from reading stale data, the system invalidates the cache line that holds the variable when a shared variable changes. This forces all the threads to read data from memory, slowing down their executions. This is called *cache coherency*. Each cache line holds many variables, which can lead to a behavior called *false sharing*, where the cache is invalidated because a widely read variable or a widely written variable sits in the same cache line, although the latter is never read.[5]

Handling such conditions is difficult. Unless you are one of the rare breeds of programmers who thrive in complexity, you won't enjoy this. The good news is that for Java and C++, the LMAX Disruptor library handles the complexity of exchanging data between threads, which you can reuse. Also, you can replace data structures shared between threads with concurrent

---

3. If you're curious about the Single Writer Principle, see https://mechanical-sympathy.blogspot.com/2011/09/single-writer-principle.html.

4. See the article "Scalability! But at What COST?" by Frank McSherry at http://www.frankmcsherry.org/graph/scalability/cost/2015/01/15/COST.html and the blog at http://blog.acolyer.org/2015/06/05/scalability-but-at-what-cost/.

5. See the blog posts at https://mechanical-sympathy.blogspot.com/2011/07/false-sharing.html and https://mechanical-sympathy.blogspot.com/2011/07/memory-barriersfences.html.

data structures. (e.g., Java concurrent data structures). Still, sometimes nothing works, and a single thread outperforms multiple threads.

Efficiently Saving Local State

Sometimes services need to save and recover a local state to or from a disk or a database, for example. In most such cases, clients need to know that the state is saved. With databases, we can achieve this with transactions. However, sometimes we use disks or queues for better performance or for more control over reliability guarantees.

Given a service that does not have randomness (a.k.a. a deterministic service), we can reconstruct its state by recording and replaying all its inputs (including timer interrupts). The reason is that a deterministic service's output depends only on its input. The following sections describe two techniques that use this principle by saving all incoming messages to a disk or to a queue so that if the service fails, it can reconstruct the state from stored messages.

Disk-Based Persistent Service

A disk-based persistent service saves each request and acknowledges its receipt to the client. This enables the service to ensure it always processes messages it receives. This behavior is a useful tool to ensure that messages are not lost while processing. However, writing each message to disk one by one is slow. Instead, as Figure 11.6 illustrates, we can keep a write queue and submit all write requests to this queue.

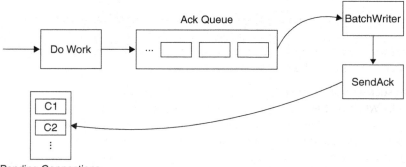

Figure 11.6
Architecture for a disk-based persistent service.

In the figure, a single thread (running batch writer) reads as many write requests as possible from the write queue (shown as the Ack queue in the figure) and writes them, batching multiple requests in a single write. When the writer has written the messages, it sends acknowledgments back to the corresponding clients. This approach lets us acknowledge each message after writing to disk when using a batch I/O, significantly improving throughput. Although simple, this method can provide 10 to 100 times better performance than writing messages one by one.

Message Queue-Based Persistent Service

In a message queue-based persistent service, the client places messages in a message queue (e.g., Apache Kafka), and the service reads from the queue and processes the messages. From time to time, the service saves its current state together with the last message ID processed. In case of a failure, the service reloads the saved state and reprocesses the last message ID. This approach enables the service to save its state periodically, not for every message, and still recover from failures, providing much better performance.

In most cases, the message queue-based service is preferred over the disk-based persistent service. The reason is that it significantly reduces the complexity of the code that we need to write.

Choosing a Transport System

Most services use HTTP as a transport mechanism to receive and send responses, but other alternatives are possible. With HTTP, the request starts from the client, the server processes the request and sends a response, and the client waits until a response is received. HTTP, however, provides no message delivery guarantees. Other transport systems include

- WebSocket, GRPC, and HTTP2. These systems can connect and hold the connection, and the server can also push messages to the client.

- Messaging protocols such as AMQP (Advanced Message Queuing Protocol) and Kafka. These protocols can send one-way (request-only) messages persistently and delete the message only after the receiver has acknowledged that processing is complete. If the receiver or message broker fails, the system can recover the messages from the disk.

My recommendation is to stick with HTTP or HTTP2 because they are widely understood and supported by most frameworks. When higher processing guarantees (e.g., guaranteed delivery and exactly once) are needed, we can use other messaging protocols: GRPC is used when we need high performance; and WebSockets, GRPC, and HTTP2 push notifications are often used when the server wants to notify the client about an event.

Handling Latency

Services often need to keep within latency bounds. Sometimes, the application has enough freedom within these bounds that special handling is not required. Chapter 3 discussed how to provide strong latency guarantees in other cases.

Separating Reads and Writes

Typical service implementations are optimized for read performance. When we need maximum write performance, it is possible to separate reads and writes into two services, as Figure 11.7 shows.

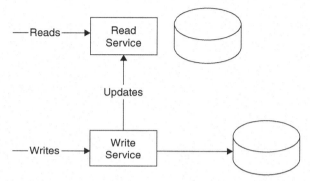

Figure 11.7
Architecture for separating reads and writes.

This approach creates a service for read operations and a service for write operations, each backed by its own database. As in Figure 11.7, all writes are directly written and sent to the read service, which constructs a model for use in the read service while responding to any queries. This model can be implemented in memory or in a database.

This approach frees the writer from read locks and from any limits on append operations. Append operations significantly reduce the need to seek delays from database operations. The resulting system can operate much faster, providing outstanding write performance. An example of this approach is CQRS (Command and Query Responsibility Segregation).[6]

We must use this approach carefully because it is tough to get this right. For example, a problem that can get us into trouble is the reconstruction of the current state from events, which can break if some code in the system is updated. To get proper state reconstruction from events, we need to track code changes and process the code using the appropriate version. Such problems are hard to fix and even harder to anticipate.

Using Locks (and Signaling) in Applications

Sometimes a service needs to coordinate the execution of its threads using locks to protect shared data structures or using semaphores to make threads wait for each other. We call constructs such as locks and semaphores *synchronization primitives*.[7]

---

6. See https://martinfowler.com/bliki/CQRS.html

7. An excellent introduction to these primitives is *The Little Book of Semaphores* by Allen B. Downey (Green Tea Press, 2009). You can find it at https://greenteapress.com/wp/semaphores/.

We should avoid coordination if possible. For example, instead of protecting data structures using locks, we can use concurrent data structures that do not need protection. Instead of using the semaphores method `acquire()`, which blocks, we can use the `tryAcquire()` method and retry if it fails. Note that we need to account for the complexity of asynchronous programming with `tryAcquire()`.

We must reduce the time execution spends with synchronization by releasing the lock or synchronization primitive as soon as possible. Consider a thread on which other threads are blocking. We should be extra careful if such a thread is doing I/O operations, performing synchronized operations, or acquiring objects from a pool. If we do these types of operations, until that thread finishes execution, none of the waiting lines can run, effectively creating a bottleneck. These kinds of bugs have cascading effects, slowing down everything. Because operations such as I/O take time, they intensify the effects of synchronization operations.

In the multicore era, where most applications use multiple cores, synchronization primitives significantly impair performance. We can explain this using Amdahl's law, as we discussed in Chapter 3. Because synchronization primitives have a crippling effect on performance, we should first tune synchronization operations before tuning other things.

If we do use synchronization, we should use a profiler to understand its behavior and optimize that, and we should do this before any other tuning. Many profilers (including Oracle's JVM profiler, Flight Recorder) include a synchronization and locks check that lets you analyze where most of the blocking happens.

Figure 11.8 shows a snapshot of thread states in a program. The lowest band shows running threads, the next shows blocked threads and the third band shows waiting threads, and the top band shows parked threads. We want the blocked threads of the program to be as small as possible. Once we know there's a problem, we can use the lock profile to find primitives that create the most overhead.

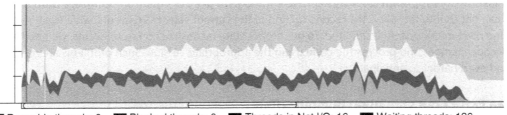

■ Runnable threads: 0   ■ Blocked threads: 0   ■ Threads in Net I/O: 16   ■ Waiting threads: 136

Figure 11.8
Snapshot of an application's thread states: running, blocked, waiting, and parked (from bottom to top, respectively).

Using Queues and Pools

We use queues to match the speed of different parts of the program. For example, if some requests come faster than we can handle, we queue them. A program using a queue can block in two ways: putting data into a full queue or reading data from an empty queue.

Queues are a significant source of latency in a system. A blocked queue behaves similarly to a synchronization primitive, and the same best practices for those apply to queues also.

Database and thread pools in our programs let us reuse something. For example, a database connection pool lets us reuse database connections, or a thread pool lets us share threads. Pools also behave similarly to a queue. It is important to note that pools are often a form of throttling to control the load on the server. For example, a thread pool controls the number of threads created, or a database connection pool controls the number of concurrent requests on the backend server.

Handling pools is not as simple as extending its pool size. We often also need to scale its backend (e.g., database). We must carefully monitor pools, and as with synchronization, we should understand the effect of pools and queues and tune them before tuning other parts of the program. At runtime, if the queue or a pool is blocked, the best practice is to propagate an error back to the client. We call this applying back pressure. We discuss this issue more fully in Chapter 12.

Handling Service Calls

Service calls (also called API calls) within code are common in new architectures. If service calls are blocked, they behave similarly to pools or locks, and they can be a severe bottleneck, as discussed previously. Because service calls always do I/O operations, handling them takes time, and the effects may be worse than queues and locks. However, often they can be handled efficiently using asynchronous I/O.

Using These Techniques in Practice

This section explores how to combine the techniques mentioned in this chapter when designing services. We already discussed the effect of locks, thread pools, and queues. However, their effects are much more dominating and predictable than the interplay between I/O, memory, and CPU. Hence, we should first tune locks, pools, and queues before tuning I/O, memory, and the CPU.

Tuning I/O, memory, and the CPU is complicated. To understand the trio, let's start with a classification of applications based on their resource usage. When an application executes, it always needs a CPU and some memory. In the following classifications, CPU and memory are always present. Because I/O is much more expensive than CPU or memory operations (see Chapter 3), even the presence of a little I/O significantly transforms the behavior of an application.

The four classifications that we explore in detail are as follows. In the following sections, we also discuss what kind of architecture suits each. Here, >> means *significantly greater than*.

- CPU-bound applications (CPU >> Memory and no I/O)

- Memory-bound applications (CPU + Bound Memory and no I/O)

- Balanced applications (CPU + Memory + I/O)
- I/O-bound applications (I/O > CPU)

CPU-Bound Applications (CPU >> Memory and No I/O)

CPU-bound applications use a lot of CPU, a little memory, and no I/O. Often, special applications such as scientific simulation or 3D rendering and brute-force attacks to crack a key follow this pattern. For example, given a number, finding the largest prime number smaller than the given number is a CPU-bound application.

Optimized architecture for this service maintains a pool of threads of the same number as CPU cores, handling a nonblocking I/O service that submits each request to one of the threads. Any surplus tasks are queued until a thread is free. To further optimize performance, we can consider pinning threads to cores, which reduces the context switch overhead. Because there is no blocking or I/O, the thread-per-request model discussed in this chapter is sufficient for this use case.

Memory-Bound Applications (CPU + Bound Memory and No I/O)

The typical architecture of memory-bound applications works similarly to CPU-bound applications, but the architect's challenges are to reduce cache misses and to optimize memory management. Because there is no blocking or I/O, the thread-per-request model is sufficient for this use case. One key concern is overhead added by cache coherency when multiple threads are working on the same data, which we already discussed in this chapter.

After cache coherency is handled, if present, the next common bottleneck is garbage collection (GC). We can use memory and object creation profiles to find problems and fix them using code changes or tuning the GC algorithm. If GC becomes a significant factor, we should consider off-heap memory management. Refer to Chapter 3 for more details.

In some cases, systems must manage a large amount of memory while processing data. Examples of these systems are databases, in-memory databases, and graph processing systems. Generally, these systems build complex indexes to avoid having to walk through all the data for processing, thus trading memory for processing. If there is excess memory, this is the right approach. Sometimes, the system may recalculate things as needed rather than storing them to trade excess CPU for storage or I/O.

Balanced Applications (CPU + Memory + I/O)

Most services (perhaps, 90%) that we write are balanced applications. When I/O presents, it adds significant complications. Threads block while doing I/O, which takes 1,000 to 2,500 times more latency than memory access (see model 2 in Chapter 3). If the CPU can't be used for the alternative task while doing I/O, it wastes the CPU. There are several ways to solve this problem.

The easiest is to add more threads (often 20–50 times the number of cores). When one thread blocks, the OS parks the blocked thread and runs a different thread, letting it use the CPU until I/O finishes. Although this approach helps, it also increases context switches, increasing the overhead added by the OS (see model 3 in Chapter 3).

As discussed previously in the section "Event-Driven (Nonblocking) Architecture," an alternative is to use the event-based model with nonblocking I/O. Nonblocking I/O checks the status of the I/O channel and issues the call only when the channel can carry out the operation. It schedules the I/O operation and releases the calling thread, which can do some other useful work meanwhile. Netty and Apache MINA are frameworks that support this model.

Unfortunately, not all calls can be nonblocking. For example, APIs provided by the most widely used database systems are blocking. In this case, both the threads and events can be used together. The SEDA architecture we discussed earlier in this chapter is an example of this model.

Sometimes, although CPU is available, the data needed for computations is not available because I/O takes a much longer time. To work around this issue, we should use the techniques described under "I/O Optimization Techniques" in Chapter 3: send early, receive late, don't ask but tell; prefetching; avoiding I/O; and buffering.

I/O-Bound Applications (I/O + Memory > CPU)

A typical architecture for the I/O-bound applications category optimizes I/O and uses other resources (e.g., CPU and memory) to reduce the required I/O. Techniques for such architectures are discussed in Chapter 3 in the section regarding optimization techniques.

Other Application Categorizations

I/O, memory, and CPU-bound categorizations reflect how a computer system works, yet we do not think about systems on those terms. Hence, the categorizations previously mentioned are limiting. Instead, we often think about an application in terms of the task performed by the service. The following sections describe two common types of services we often encounter.

Calculators

Calculators carry out computations. The design revolves around making data available to make those calculations as fast as possible. There are several use cases for this:

- **Case 1:** If applications have readily available data, it becomes a CPU-bound, no I/O application. Examples include calculating prime numbers or breaking a password.

- **Case 2:** If computations need a lot of memory access, it becomes a memory-bound application. Examples include scientific simulations such as weather forecasting or air tunnel simulation.

- **Case 3:** If data comes through I/O, the application has to do a lot of work to move data and make it available for computations. An example is big data applications such as MapReduce. I/O optimization techniques such as prefetching and batching also can help a lot in these situations.

  Often the resulting application would be I/O-bound because a bottleneck would bring in the data. Thus, it becomes a balanced application (CPU + Memory + I/O).

Also, these three cases reveal a pattern that we often see. The main goal of the application and the real bottlenecks of the implementation can be different.

Update and Lookup Services

Most applications that look up data run as servers. Among examples are relational databases, NoSQL databases such as Cassandra and MongoDB, and both time series and graph databases. They often support complex query languages such as SQL. Two types of databases, based on where they store the data, are memory or disk. Both cases use indexes to find data, which may also be stored in memory or on disk.

Although trivial implementations of these systems are I/O or memory-bound, most real-world implementations use the CPU to trade off I/O operations. For example, Cassandra stores data in SSTables, which are append-only, where they achieve higher I/O bandwidth but have to combine multiple updates on demand to get the current value to support a read operation. This means giving up computations to optimize I/O. Complex update and lookup services often become balanced applications after optimizations.

Leadership Considerations

When creating services, developers need to understand the business requirements, typically expressed as "business logic," and quality of service (QoS) requirements. Leaders have to make sure that these business contexts are factored into the API design, shared with the developers, and integrated into testing processes.

Three usual errors while creating services are

- Making premature optimizations
- Not paying enough attention to APIs
- Not tuning the service first before changing the macro architecture

As we've mentioned, creating services is pretty straightforward with modern service development tools. They use a thread-per-request model, which is easy to manage and understand. Often, only a few services in the macro architecture affect overall performance. So it's an error to move away from the default structure in a service before we know it's truly the bottleneck.

Second, API definitions are part of the macro architecture and should be designed carefully because they're hard to change. Yet, it's common for architects to hand over the API details to the development team because they know the specifics. Architects need to keep an eye on this issue, review, and make sure these APIs are designed carefully and the risk of big changes is small. Good APIs greatly cut down the risk linked with the service. Poorly designed APIs can lead to expensive changes throughout the system.

Third, when a service is the bottleneck, detailed tuning can sometimes lead to major improvements. It's an error to scale the macro architecture before tuning the server architecture to achieve maximum performance. For example, let's say we need to deliver 12,000 TPS and each service can deliver 1,000 TPS. But, with careful tuning, sometimes a single service can provide 15,000 TPS, which would greatly simplify the overall structure. It's important to explore this possibility before changing the macro architecture.

Lastly, the skills needed for server architectures are often different from those needed for macro architecture. Great server developers are skilled in dealing with concurrency and have a deep understanding of how computers work in detail. You should aim to have a few experienced server developers in your team to help when you deviate from the thread-per-request model.

Summary

Following are key takeaways from this chapter:

- Writing services is relatively easy using modern service development frameworks. These use the thread-per-request model, which is simple to support and to understand.

- Here are some of the best practices in writing services: when making services stateless, try not to block the threads, makes operations idempotent, and control both the client and service if you can.

- You can perform better than a de facto service with event-driven or SEDA models, but the resulting implementations are much more complex to code, debug, and maintain. If you choose to go with sophisticated techniques, it is a good idea to add people to the team who have handled such designs and implementations before.

- You should first tune locks, pools, and service calls before profiling your service.

- I/O, CPU, and memory in an application have a complex relationship. Based on the type of bottleneck, you can trade one to save another. For example, applications can trade memory to save CPU by using a cache.

- It is easier to tune individual services than to tune the whole system.

- You need to balance the cost of the complexity in the services against the cost of complexity in the macro architecture to scale the system.

12

Building Stable Systems

Clever architects achieve scalability. Yet, the stability of their systems separates great architects from good ones. A stable system is predictable, fulfilling the specifications of the system under varying conditions and degrading gradually if the system faces extraordinary circumstances. After a system meets its specifications, stability is the fundamental expectation from the system. Stability encompasses maintaining aspects such as fault tolerance, high availability, scalability within its specifications, even when the system receives external shocks (e.g., workload changes, failures). A stable system is economical, gives peace of mind, and empowers the team to evolve the design. In this chapter, we explore how to build a stable system.

Why Do Systems Fail, and What Can We Do About Them?

What do we mean by stability? Many equate it to high availability (HA). I believe availability is only a part of the problem. The first goal of the system is never to get into an irreversible or inconsistent state and never to cause significant harm. The second goal is to be available as much as possible. For example, consider two systems. First is a single-node system with a backup that is unavailable for a small time frame until it is recovered after failing. The second is a two-node system that might corrupt the database in edge cases. The former is preferred over the latter.

Note that the stability of a system goes beyond avoiding failures. Any system can and will fail, but stable systems can recover faster with minimal interruptions to the system. Refusing to accept this and overreaching to avoid failures lead to longer downtimes and catastrophes. For example, adopting complex data replication systems increases the risk of corrupting the data storage due to unforeseen failure scenarios. Take Figure 12.1, for example.

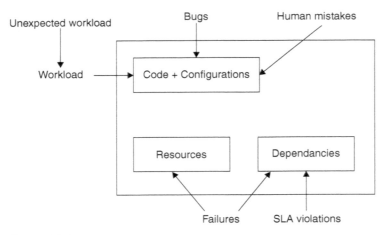

Figure 12.1
Factors affecting the stability of the system.

What affects the stability of a system? As Figure 12.1 shows, code, configurations, resources, dependencies, and workload affect the system. Surprises related to each can affect the stability. The following are examples of scenarios that affect stability:

- Unexpected workloads

    - High load

    - High concurrency

    - Load fluctuations

    - Unexpected inputs

    - DOS attacks

    - Security attacks

    - Slow clients

- Resource and dependency failures, plus service-level agreement violations

    - Machine failures

    - Network failures

    - Database failures

    - Slow nodes (database)

    - DNS failures

    - Authentication failures

    - Slow DNS

- Network partitions

- Out-of-memory (OOM) errors

- Disk over capacity

- CPU-consuming processes

- Clock out of sync

- Human mistakes

  - Code changes

  - Configuration mistakes

- Software bugs in both ours and borrowed code

We can anticipate and avoid or recover from as many known errors as possible. However, when avoidance or recovery is not possible, the system should capture as much information as possible so that we can fix the problem and avoid any recurrence. The rest of the chapter discusses different approaches to handle conditions that lead to instability. Then, we discuss unknown failures and how to detect and address them.

How to Handle Known Errors

The following sections discuss how to handle common types of known errors. They include unexpected load, resource failures, dependencies, and human changes.

Handling Unexpected Load

The workload the system receives can go beyond its specifications. This can happen because the business organization is doing well due to a temporary peak or to a denial-of-service (DoS) attack. In either case, if not carefully handled, a system can have terrible latencies due to the higher load. We must be concerned about this when any system operates close to its limits.

First, we need to understand the load and set up a system that can keep up with the load most of the time. This is called *capacity planning*. Although autoscaling reduces the need for capacity planning, we still need to tune the autoscaling algorithm (e.g., how many warm nodes to keep) based on average capacity. Also, my experience is that the gains we get by running too close to the system's limit are negated by complexity and effort to recover from performance issues. Thus, we are better off adding extra resources and leaving a buffer.

Recall from Chapter 3 how a system behaves under load. We can think of any system or service as a queuing system, where work is placed in queues and one or more workers process the work and produce a response. When there are no explicit queues, work will block and wait in the OS queues (CPU queue, I/O queue, etc.) until it can be processed. Because of these queues, we can use queuing theory to understand systems and the latency of a system, as Figure 12.2 depicts.

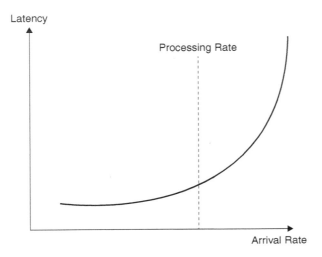

Figure 12.2
Latency vs. arrival rate.

As Figure 12.2 shows, queues have a trigger behavior with latency. As long as the arrival rate is the same as or less than the processing rate, latency is fairly stable, but once the arrival rate exceeds the processing rate, latency shoots through the roof. This is bad news if a service or a system receives requests that far exceed expectations: latency skyrockets, and the system becomes unusable in practice. When the higher load is received, we have only a little time to recover.

Autoscaling

What can we do? One option is autoscaling. We can create more workers (e.g., service replicas) to handle the load. However, starting a new service and getting it to work takes some time. We must begin to autoscale before the problem intensifies. A typical approach is to keep a buffer of nodes live and proactively start autoscaling. Sometimes, however, autoscaling is not possible. Even when autoscaling is possible, we can't autoscale forever (we hit a different bottleneck). Additionally, it is possible to receive a load beyond the limits of autoscaling.

When facing a high load, if we can't handle it by autoscaling, then the only alternative is to drop requests. This is a heated and highly contested topic. Many would argue that we can't drop user requests. However, the truth is that we are faced with dropping a few requests versus dropping most of them when latency inevitably spikes.

If we take more requests than we can handle, the queue grows, and future requests must wait longer. Soon requests in the queue start to time out. We then need to take corrective measures.

Admission Control

We can use admission control (also known as *load shredding*) to handle load spikes. For example, when a video streaming service found that its payments service couldn't keep up with the demand during a launch, they handled payment service rejections by giving customers the first month free. This solution makes sense because customer acquisition costs (CACs) in video services are often much higher than the first month's subscription fee.

Another critical advantage of admission control is predictability, which isolates load problems and handles them as early as possible. Furthermore, admission control significantly improves the latency of the system.

We can implement admission control through either a request timeout or using a queue length limit. With the former method, we reject requests that have taken more than a timeout value. With the latter method, the system rejects new requests if the queue length is too large or growing too fast. When there is no queue, we can use the number of messages *in flight* (messages received by the service, but those that are not done yet) to measure the queue length. We can do this with a simple counter. Between the two methods, the latter is more efficient because the former uses up system resources before rejecting the requests. It is also possible to use both methods in tandem, providing greater stability.

My recommendation is to always operate each service at about 80% of its capacity, leaving room for absorbing any surprises. When the queue length is too high (or if the queue length is growing too fast), we should reject the requests and retry at the load balancer level or at the client, which buys the system time to recover. If that fails, the system must notify the user to drop the request (and maybe give them a coupon to compensate).

If we use more advanced admission control algorithms such as machine learning, it may be possible to operate the service closer to its limits. However, my recommendation is to start with a simple algorithm (queue length) that you can use as the baseline against more advanced algorithms. Then use advanced algorithms only when they can significantly outperform (> 50%) the baseline.

When a downstream service in a cascade of services is experiencing a load spike, the service must propagate an error back to the services before them. Typically, this is done by sending an error or HTTP code such as 503 – Service Unavailable. This is called *back pressure*. Back pressure propagates through the call path and eventually asks the client to slow down (or the client program automatically does this). If we don't use back pressure, the requests stack up in the service, slowing down the server, and the server eventually dies (typically causing an out-of-memory error).

In addition to allowing the system to keep working and autoscale without failing, the most significant advantage of back pressure is to avoid out-of-memory errors, which are usually hard to isolate and fix. Instead, back pressure creates overloaded errors whose root cause is evident, opening the possibility of automatic recovery.

Noncritical Functionality

Another useful tool in handling load is to turn off noncritical functionality. A classic example already discussed is an online retailer skipping charges for small transactions. Turning off noncritical functionality is typically an advanced feature that we should add to a system after exhausting other avenues to handle the increased load.

We can simulate most load conditions and test the system, which helps us understand the system deeply. Furthermore, systematic and detailed data collection and analysis (e.g., the number of messages in flight for each service in the system) further deepen our understanding.

Finally, workloads can sometimes create unexpected situations. A great example is slow clients. Years back, while debugging a production outage, we saw the throughput of enterprise service buses (ESBs) gradually deteriorating in a critical client deployment, and after weeks of investigation, we found that the culprit was slow clients. In this case, some clients talking to the system were behind a slow network (mobile phone), and reading from and writing to those clients blocked worker threads in the ESB, effectively reducing the number of effective threads in the ESB. Such problems are hard to detect and only found through careful analysis. Note that full nonblocking architectures are resilient against these types of specific slow clients.

Sometimes, the higher load can come as an attack (called a DoS attack). Although having proper overload limits can prevent the system from failing, DOS can still stop legitimate users from getting their work done. As we discussed before, DOS needs special techniques, which we find in most firewalls.

I recommend setting up overload limits both at each node level and at the overall load balancer cluster level. Node-level overload limits protect the node if the load is not distributed evenly among the cluster and enable the node to handle the problem, returning when the failure is resolved. When we use autoscaling, we should adjust the load balancer overload limit based on the currently active nodes.

Handling Resource Failures

External shock is a fact of life. Computers, disks, and even networks can fail. Some failures are total and complex to recover from, needing human interactions. Examples are a failed or slow DNS server, an out-of-sync clock, a failed network, or expired certificates. To handle such situations, we create processes and, sometimes, have dedicated people to monitor and avoid failures in such critical infrastructures. Observability alerts can also help to focus site reliability engineering (SRE) on potential problems.

We try to recover from these problems automatically. There are two key approaches. The first is building systems that never fail, and the second is building systems that can recover quickly, which we discussed in Chapter 9.

Considering replication, when a service fails and the system switches to a replica, it no longer has a backup. We need to notify operations teams so that they fix the problem and recover the failed service, restoring a replica into the system. The following discussion focuses on a fast recovery in such situations. However, the fast recovery of a database is often complicated due to state. It is recommended to perform active or passive replication (see Chapter 9) using tools provided by the database. I recommend fast recovery methods as much as possible for the rest of the system because they make the overall system more stable. We need to meet the following conditions to use fast recovery:

- Services need to be stateless.

- Startup time of individual services is low (2–3 seconds).

- Services can start and join the system in any order.

As part of services and macro architecture design, we should try to meet these conditions.

If we have fast recovery, when a node fails, other nodes that depend on the failed node need to switch to a replacement. There are several ways to achieve this:

- We can reroute all service calls between services through a load balancer, which detects service failures and reroutes the traffic to the replica.

- As discussed in Chapter 9, some network layers let us hot-swap IPs, and if that is available, the system can detect service failures and swap the IPs.

- Each service can detect failures and reconnect to a replica. The service can get replicas from configurations or a central registry.

While the switch happens, the failed service is unavailable. When a service detects that its downstream resources are unavailable, it needs to retry. For a short time, it can retry to see whether downstream services will become available. However, if a problem persists, it should try to find a replica when possible. If that is not possible, the client propagates the error back to upstream services, allowing it to reroute traffic or notify the end user. At the same time after a permanent failure, the system needs to resend requests when the service comes back online. A typical approach is for upstream services to periodically ping the failed service and add it back to active replicas when it becomes available. Even when the replica resides in the same address as the old service, the client may get an error. Then the client may need to log in again, reestablish sessions, and reset connection pools.

We need to automate parts of the system that use fast recovery. Having a human in the loop adds at least a 15–30-minute delay, severely reducing availability. In a cloud platform, we can use Kubernetes, serverless, or equivalent features for recovery.

Detection of Resource Failures

Both fast recovery and replication depend on detecting failures. However, detecting the failure of resources is not perfect. False negatives (not detecting the error) are usually not a significant concern because, with time, the system will detect the failure if it persists. However, we always need to ask what happens if a false positive occurs (detecting an error when there is no error). Let's consider a few examples.

If a node fails, Kubernetes restarts it. However, if a restart does not fix the problem, the node gets into a restart/fail loop. The slow or overloaded network sometimes leads to false positives and a random restart of systems due to a recovery loop. For example, default CPU thresholds in Kubernetes can create this situation with CPU-hungry services. It is a good idea to detect restart loops and shut down the offending system or the whole system based on the blast radius.

If failure detection is a false positive, some services may switch to the replica, although others may continue with the primary. Furthermore, even when the secondary takes over due to a detected failure, the primary can continue to work. As happened in the well-documented case of the Knight Capital Group, two nodes, being active in an active-passive setup simultaneously, created problems. Because of this, Knight Capital lost millions of dollars in one day.[1] A database lock, discussed in the next section, is one way to avoid two active nodes in an active-passive setup.

The best defense against these cases is a careful analysis of edge cases and comprehensive testing. It is also important to generate events when the system topology undergoes changes so that the SRE team can check and guard against edge cases. Additionally, it is often a good idea to independently monitor the work being done and use that to trigger alerts. For example, if the transaction rate is lower than average in a bank, it is a good idea to generate an alert, triggering administrator oversight.

Furthermore, failures are often rare; thus, recovery paths rarely run. Therefore, if recovery paths are broken, we would not know about that situation until it's too late. It is a good idea to conduct drills that simulate failures to test the recovery path. An advanced version of this approach is called *Chaos Monkey*, which is a process that randomly injects failures into the system, forcing it to recover, making sure recovery paths work.

Finally, if the data does not change quickly and is not very big (e.g., configuration data), sometimes it is useful to keep cache values and fall back on those values if the source is unavailable. For example, when a service loads configurations from a config registry, it can maintain a configuration cache to allow it to work even if the configuration registry fails. This useful pattern increases the system's stability across the board.

---

1. See https://www.henricodolfing.com/2019/06/project-failure-case-study-knight-capital.html

Network Partitions

Network partitions are a special case of resource failures, and they may be the most complex challenge in distributed systems. A network partition breaks the network into two fully disconnected partitions, and when this happens, each partition thinks that nodes in the other partitions are dead. Both partitions can proceed to serve user requests, putting the system in an inconsistent state. Also, when partitions are resolved, the systems in the two partitions must merge.

The typical approach for a network partition is to use a quorum, where the partition with more than half of the nodes continues while the other side gives up and waits. Because only one partition can have more than half the nodes, this approach works. However, a quorum is possible only if we have at least three copies and an odd number of nodes.

With two nodes, we can approximate a solution with each node getting a database lock, allowing whatever partition that includes the database to continue. However, with this technique, the system fails if the database fails, which is a single point of failure that needs to be handled separately. We used this technique in a message broker product that I designed.

Regardless of the approach, it is a good idea to get a human involved as soon as possible. Then, when possible, it is easier to wipe out the system and restart rather than merging the two partitioned systems.

With new network hardware, network partitions are rare. Also, if you have a typical system with stateless services and a database without automatic failover, network partitions aren't harmful because, usually, only one side hosts the database. When you set up automatic failover, you need to be careful because two databases can continue on their own.

Look out for network partitions. Especially check them if you are using a complicated architecture because then the potential damage of network partitions is much higher.

Handling Dependencies

With the cloud and API economy, our systems depend on other systems. As Leslie Lamport reports:

> *A distributed system is one in which the failure of a computer you didn't even know existed can render your own computer unusable.*[2]

Lamport's quote is accurate for many systems. Dependencies are either at the infrastructure level or at the service level. We use cloud hardware (IaaS, or Infrastructure as a Service) or platforms (PaaS, or Platform as a Service) at the infrastructure level, and we use a network service or APIs provided as SaaS (Software as a Service) at the service level.

---

2. https://en.wikiquote.org/wiki/Leslie_Lamport

Our availability can never be higher than our dependencies. The first question is, "Is the availability of our dependencies sufficient?" Most systems aim to support three to four 9s of availability, while cloud infrastructures often provide four to five 9s of availability. Hence, often, we do not need to worry about cloud infrastructure availability.

The availability of APIs (services) varies widely. When service providers promise penalties if they fall short of a service-level agreement (SLA), it is a sign of stability, but we should make sure penalties represent risks. However, the availability of most APIs provided by cloud providers is often high enough and sufficient. If we need higher infrastructure availability than that provided by cloud providers, we must run a parallel system with another cloud provider.

I recommend that, at the system's initial rollout, availability provided by most dependencies is sufficient. The added complexity of ultra-high availability is often not justifiable. As your app finds more adoption, you'll need to make a decision on how to proceed. It is important to keep track of the availability of your dependencies and whether they live up to their promises. If service providers are falling short, escalate early. Their response tells you important information about their reliability as partners. We will need alternative APIs to reduce the risk due to API-level dependencies. Also, it is important to think through what happens if dependencies are down. It is much better to stop serving requests than to lose customer requests, fail them in the last step, or worse, take the system to a corrupted state.

Furthermore, two common problems we face are running out of quota and high tail latencies. Let's consider each in detail. At design and deployment time, we need to ensure that the system can operate within the quota given by the service provider. We must use back pressure and fail gracefully if running out of quota while generating alerts, for instance. Clear error propagation can save a lot of time. With tail latencies, we need to work with the service provider. There are solutions, such as sending two parallel requests and then using the first response (which works only with idempotent operations), but then you consume the quota twice as fast. In both of these cases, if the service provider says no, we do not have a good recourse other than moving away and finding another provider.

It is important to do back-of-the-napkin calculations to ensure we are not operating at the edge or beyond the limits. If we operate at the edge, or in other words, our system is performance-sensitive, we need to evaluate the choice of external dependencies carefully.

Handling Human Changes

Finally, let's explore stability against the changes we make. Unfortunately, changes we make are a common source of system downtimes. Let's look at how we can mitigate those mistakes.

The first defense is to check all changes against a test setup. The test setup is a parallel setup that duplicates the production conditions as closely as possible. We must push all new changes to the test setup and run exhaustive tests before applying the changes to production. The quality of this step depends on the quality of the tests.

Another powerful tool is GitOps, which keeps all information required to boot up the system in a version-controlled repository (e.g., Git). Often, you can apply the same patch you applied to a test setup to the production GitOps repository, reducing the chance of typos. With GitOps, we can boot up a parallel copy and switch traffic when a failure happens. However, preserving the database state in the switch is complicated. The common solution is to have a highly available database setup and use GitOps with the rest of the system.

The next idea is to have blue-green systems where we keep two systems live, called *blue* and *green*. When we want to change the system, we make another copy, apply changes, test, and then switch traffic. We keep the original system as a backup in case of failures. Like before, it is not practical to sync data quickly between two databases. Therefore, both systems must share the same database.

Canary deployments are the next evolution of this model. A canary deployment lets us test the new system under realistic conditions and switch to contain the impact of a potential failure. In a canary setup, we send a small percentage of users to the new system and gradually increase the load to that system as it proves itself, finally crossing over to the new system entirely. In some real-life deployments, complete crossovers can take months.

Common Bugs

A few common failures can happen within system design or implementation. Let us explore two: resource leaks and deadlocks.

Resource Leaks

A memory leak can cause system memory to grow and eventually crash. Even with garbage collection, memory leaks are possible. Objects referenced from long-running or static objects are not cleaned, and they can lead to memory leaks. Leaks can also happen in connection pools, file descriptors, other pools, and so on.

We typically check for leaks through long-running tests. Although it is possible to catch leaks in the common path through long-running tests, this approach does not detect leaks in less common paths. We should watch our servers for leaks through observability metrics. If we observe any leaks, we should collect as much information as possible before restarting the system. The reason is that some leaks are hard to recreate.

With container-based systems, another drastic approach is to reboot all services periodically (using a round-robin restart) to avoid any subtle leaks from building up. For example, the Apache Server destroys each process after some time to reduce the effect of memory leaks. With containers, we can now do this with any code.

Deadlocks and Slow Operations

Deadlocks block threads and take them out of usual processing, which can lead to slower response times or timeouts. Deadlocks are hard to detect and find because they occur rarely. Often, they happen when the code acquires an exclusive lock or a resource while holding other exclusive resources. Also, not all blocks that cause deadlocks are apparent because some locks might be inside a database query and out of our control. I recommend reading *The Little Book of Semaphores* by Allen B. Downey (Green Tea Press, 2009) to understand deadlocks.

To prevent deadlocks, it is best practice to avoid acquiring one resource while holding the other. If you must do this, all code segments need to acquire the resources in the same order. For example, consider the following code:

```
locka =
lockb =

Thread 1:
    locka.aquire()
    do_work(..)
    lockb.aquire()
    do_work()
    lockb.release()
    locka.release()

Thread 2:
    lockb.aquire()
    do_work(..)
    locka.aquire()
    do_work()
    locka.release()
    lockb.release()
```

If Thread 2 acquires `lockb` after Thread 1 acquires `locka`, we have a deadlock. If in Thread 2 we move `locka.aquire()` as the first statement, then a deadlock is not possible because if we get locka, it is guaranteed that `lockb` is available. Yet, in complex systems, it is often hard to ensure the order of resource allocations.

When possible, we should avoid deadlocks by acquiring resources in the same order. If not, long-running tests with many participants might recreate the deadlocks, helping us in finding and fixing them.

Timeouts also help with deadlocks, but before a timeout happens, often the system is slowed down significantly. Similar effects can happen due to slow operations. For example, performing blocking I/O when the system has only a few threads can significantly reduce its performance. Also, doing I/O while holding exclusive resources forces everyone waiting on the resources to indirectly wait on the I/O, slowing down the system. This effect is called the *Convoy Effect*.

It is good practice to use timeouts when performing potentially slow operations. Timeouts reduce the potential impact due to mistakes in the logic. However, we must log those timeouts and investigate because their occurrence signals a bug in the system.

How to Handle Unknown Errors

Unknown errors often stem from observability and bugs and testing. The following sections look at each of these situations.

Observability

Great architects know they cannot anticipate all error conditions. Architects who think otherwise are either arrogant, ignorant, or inexperienced. The more you learn about systems, the more you realize there are things that you do not know and do not understand. Therefore, wise architects learn from their system. They aim to extract all learning from the system.

The best way to do this is to observe the system deeply. The idea is to build deep metrics into the system. We can use an Application Performance Monitoring (APM) tool coupled with custom metrics such as latencies, throughputs, queue lengths, resource utilization, and so forth. We need to watch these metrics manually, using anomaly detectors (e.g., artificial intelligence). We should compare the behaviors against the expected baseline. When a system deviates, we need to explore the root causes, and if we can't, we need to improve our metrics.

Most importantly, when a failure happens, we need to be able to capture as much information as possible to enable us to find the problem and fix it. Our system needs its own black box, like an airplane. Some failures are rare and hard to recreate. Unless we have enough data, we can't fix them. To find the root cause, we need to play detective. The book *Debugging: The 9 Indispensable Rules for Finding Even the Most Elusive Software and Hardware Problems* by David J. Agans (HarperCollins Publishing, 2002) addresses this topic deeply.

Bugs and Testing

Enough has been said of the effects of bugs and how to reduce them when writing code that I will not add to that discussion here. And we know that we can catch known errors through testing. Known errors are any errors we find while testing, and we either fix or use them to define the limits of the system.

A computer program is often deterministic. In other words, given the same input, it produces the same output. Input comes in three forms: external inputs (user inputs, events, messages), internal states, and failures. If we can test the system against all possible input, then we have fully tested the system. However, often these three types of input are infinite.

The best approach is to test the system against all input classes. We identify classes and design one or more tests to verify each class. For example, one case would be if the name field is longer than 256 characters. However, often there is an infinite number of classes, so we need to consider only the important ones. We miss bugs if we leave out the important classes. For example, if we do not consider what happens if the system gets a false-positive resource failure, we might miss some bugs.

Important classes to consider are the known potential issues (known-unknowns). Our tests should convert these to known bugs so that we can either fix them or use them to identify the system's limits. Furthermore, testing guards against the recurrence of those issues. Important classes we miss are the unknown potential issues (unknown-unknowns).

I see testing as a search with two competing priorities: exploration versus exploitation. Exploitation is the discipline of comprehensively testing known-unknowns. Exploration is discovering unknown-unknowns (missed important classes) through creativity. Following are some techniques to find important classes of input:

- **Anticipate surprises:** Two approaches to this are checking the system against fallacies of distributed systems (see https://en.wikipedia.org/wiki/Fallacies_of_distributed_computing) and identifying your assumptions in your design, asking what if those are no longer true.

- **Undertake chaos testing:** Using randomness as your ally, you can inject random data and failures, and simulate random scenarios to identify error scenarios.

- **Encourage brainstorming:** Use a diverse group of people to come up with scenarios (classes) where the system can fail. The diversity of individuals helps because people in your team with different expertise, backgrounds, and upbringing contributing to the design can help find failure scenarios.

- **Use AI generators:** Recent advances in AI let you easily generate new input and combinations thereof, which you can use to test the system and uncover failure scenarios. Systems such as co-pilot and ChatGPT can also generate test cases or test scenarios.

Exploration and exploitation are well-known problems that have been widely studied. The multi-arm bandit algorithm is one approach to balance them. Some of those strategies might be useful when planning a testing strategy. Blue-green and canary tests are our last defense against unknown-unknowns. Not only do they help uncover human errors, but they also help with bugs, only if that condition occurs while testing.

Finally, having a bias toward simplicity in design helps us reduce unknown-unknowns. For example, we should use complex algorithms or designs only with extraordinary gains. We must be aware of complex situations such as acquiring a resource or doing I/O while holding a resource. Also, CQRS is a great idea, but code changes make things very complex. Simple designs make it easy to debug and recover from problems. Keeping dependency paths between services simple with less depth is also a good idea. We also should look out for cyclic dependencies.

Graceful Degradation

Once we hit the goal of avoiding disasters and improving availability, graceful degradation is a desired feature of the system. Graceful degradation can come in two ways. The first, as we discussed already, is to continue to work when the load exceeds the resources and, at least, serve a subset of users. We should use back pressure, admission control, and timeouts to avoid the whole system failing. Also, we might reject certain kinds of input.

The second approach is to continue to work with reduced functionality. The inspiration comes from bulkheads in ships, which stop the vessel from sinking even if part of it floods. An example of this is the control plane/data plane separation, where the data plane continues to work (maybe with reduced functionality) if the control plane fails.

Leadership Considerations

There are two types of instability:

- The system is not accessible for a period.

- There are unrecoverable, severe failures, like corrupting the database or losing data.

The first step is to keep both in mind. It's easy to focus on keeping the system available (the first type) and ignore the risk of the second type. Also, complex systems have a higher risk of instability.

The best way to improve stability is to have a clear model of the system you're building, with a good understanding of its limits. However, this isn't always possible, so we have to use the techniques described in this chapter. Many of these stability-enhancing methods are complex, which can actually increase instability.

We need to remember this feedback loop and know when to stop. A key part of stability is accepting low-probability failures or failures we can recover from quickly. Overreaching to prevent failures can lead to longer downtimes and catastrophes. For instance, using complex data replication systems can increase the risk of database corruption due to unforeseen failure scenarios.

As a leader, you need to understand this trade-off: Aiming for stability can also reduce your stability, and you need to find a balance that suits your context.

For example, many complex decisions come from the need for stability, so consider the second question discussed in Chapter 2: What is the skill level of the team? Can the team handle it?

If you choose a complex design, consider these points in relation to stability:

> Question 5: What are the hard problems?
>
> Principle 5: Design deeply things that are hard to change but implement them slowly.
>
> Principle 6: Eliminate the unknowns and learn from the evidence by working on hard problems early and in parallel.

Just like security, stability is relative. We should aim to achieve a level of stability within the available time and resources. As leaders, we may need to refer to the question of when we can rewrite the system and the principle of making decisions and absorbing the risks to guide the team.

An often-overlooked way to achieve stability is to run each part of the system below its limits, leaving room for unexpected events. In many cases, adding complexity is more costly in the long run than running the system close to its limits.

If the system is performance-sensitive, the risk of instability is higher, and it's a good idea to consider stability as part of the design. However, you should go for complex solutions only after careful thought.

Finally, external dependencies can pose risks to stability. But it's important to use them as much as possible, and you may need to make decisions and accept risks to enable reuse.

Summary

Following are key takeaways from this chapter:

- Stability is not equal to high availability. The first goal of the system is never to get into an irreversible, inconsistent state and not to cause significant harm. The second goal is to be available as much as possible.

- We handle unexpected workloads through autoscaling or admission control of requests.

- We handle resource failures using replication or fast recovery.

- We cannot have better availability or stability than our dependencies (e.g., cloud providers or hardware we run on, APIs we use). We must choose these carefully and then monitor them.

- We can handle human mistakes through GitOps, blue-green systems, and canary deployments.

- We can detect unknown issues through observability and testing.

- When we encounter instabilities that we can't handle, we need to reduce the impact by controlling admission, refusing specific requests, shutting down certain features, and so on.

13

Building and Evolving the Systems

This chapter discusses how to connect what we discussed throughout the book and apply those concepts to real life—from setting up the basics, designing and demanding excellence from the team, getting the best out of each member, and meeting business goals.

Getting Your Hands Dirty

In earlier parts of this book, we discussed design and leadership principles for design. We dug deep into the technical considerations while exploring key concepts and trade-offs. In this chapter, we connect the dots and discuss how to apply those concepts, focusing on breaking ground, getting things moving, and using your tools and team to sculpt the system that you see in your mind's eye.

Get the Basics Right

The first step is to get the basics right. Although the basics are well known, unfortunately, most projects have a few of them wrong. Pay attention to the basics, get them right, and ensure continuity. Following are some commonsense basics to pay attention to. These are by no means exhaustive.

To begin with, the project must have a simple build where developers can do one checkout and issue one command to create their part of the system. Make sure that the build works across all machines and that the developer's machines have enough resources to run the build fast.

Builds with unit tests should run in less than 15–20 minutes and should give the developers confidence that everything is good. If the build takes longer or unit tests do not cover key aspects, your developers will be reluctant to touch the code unless it is absolutely necessary. The reason is that without a solid way to verify changes, every time they touch the code, the developers face a tedious cycle of verifying his changes, or worse, of accepting blame for breaking the system. When this happens, the code stops evolving and starts rusting and dying.

My recommendation is to either use pair programming or review then commit model, where four eyes see every commit. The reviewer must accept responsibility for mistakes in the code, so make sure this part of the job is taken seriously. Reward good reviewers through consideration for promotions, for example, and punish sloppy reviewers as appropriate.

It is also important to make sure reviews happen promptly, and developers do not have to wait days to get reviews completed and approved. These kinds of waits add up and slow down the system, zapping the developers' enthusiasm in the long run. Team leaders need to make sure reviewers are assigned and available.

Developers should be able to write unit tests easily, but sometimes writing unit tests requires specific frameworks or tools. It is important to design those layers explicitly and to allocate time for implementation, not waiting for the developer who first needs those tests to figure it out.

You should ask developers to talk to an architect if they cannot test a certain aspect as a unit test, and architects should invest the time to find a solution when such a case is escalated. This way, you take away the developers' potential excuses not to write unit tests. If you let such loopholes open up, a few will abuse these loopholes, which will spread like a disease. Writing good unit tests takes time, and we must be ready to invest that time. Additionally, reviewers must make sure adequate unit tests are in place along with the main logic.

It is important that developers have an environment where they can easily test complicated scenarios. If your product is an SaaS product, then this environment would be a development or predevelopment environment where developers can deploy and test their changes. If your product is *not* an SaaS product, then it can be an integration test framework, or you can choose to have an internal deployment where developers can test their changes easily whenever they want.

Architects should work with a quality assurance (QA) team to identify and define integration tests. Additionally, we need to identify a subset of smoke tests for quick verification that runs periodically (e.g., every hour or every 30 minutes) so that the team knows right away if something fails.

Integration test failures present two common challenges: scenarios that are hard to automate and intermittent tests. If we ignore these challenges, a subset of the team could abuse them to avoid writing tests. My recommendation is to ask anyone to escalate whenever they face such a challenge, and an architect should work with them to resolve the challenge. I believe this step is important because it takes away the possibility of using these challenges as a way to avoid writing tests. Moreover, it sends the right message to the team.

As with unit tests, without reliable testing, when we try to move forward with the system, we will be forced to take a few steps back because changes can break the system, but we cannot know of possible breaks without unit tests. The key to success is the agility of our systems—our ability to fix things fast and get them into production.

Often, the enemy of agility is a large and heavy build, where we can get something out only when everything works, which often requires us to run a multihour build many times to get even a simple thing into production. We can show this with simple calculations.

For example, let's assume that each developer has a 1-in-100 chance to commit something that breaks the build. With 10 developers, we have to run the build 1.09 times on average before it passes, but with 100 developers, we will have to run the build 2.5 times on average. Furthermore, with more work in one build, the longer the build will take, which multiplies the time we need to take. On top of that, the more interdependent the system is, the more likely an individual will make a mistake.

As discussed in Chapter 10, the solution is to model the system as loosely coupled service groups, each owned by a team, where each team can deploy its parts independently into production. A typical way to do this is to use microservices, although sometimes it is possible to assign multiple services to a single team and ask them to deploy all of them as a single unit.

The next challenge is large features that slow down quick but important fixes. Often quick fixes are important to create a better UX because then we can identify UX bottlenecks and fix them, learning from our users. It is crucial to be able to flag important features and get them through the process quickly and into production. The test for this is to monitor the time to get a simple change (e.g., a label) into production, which will provide a ballpark figure for building your important features. This will help us provide a good UX.

Finally, we need to keep our eye on the open bug count. This is like cleaning your home: If you do not clean daily, cleaning soon becomes a multiday project. We need about 20% of the team to actively fix bugs, and we need to adjust this allocation based on the open bugs.

Basics ensure developers do not have to jump through hoops to do their job. Developers are the most expensive resource you have. Put in place the right team and get out of the way. Understand their experience while building the system. It is our job to make sure their work environment is a pleasant one.

Understand the Design Process

The first step in the design process is the roadmap. The *roadmap* lets us decide what to put into the product and what not to put into it. There is a right way and a wrong way to do this.

The wrong way is to approach the project from the point of view of the internal implementation and choose *N* easily implementable features because the architecture suggests the features. This is a bad idea! Neither program architects nor the product team should dictate the roadmap. Instead, watch and listen to the users.

Understand what users are trying to do. Focus on understanding the users' journey and then ask the question, "How can we make it better?" Some answers are simple to implement, and some answers are complex. Our focus should be on giving users a natural and simple experience.

Every project needs someone who understands the users and their journey in detail, who holds all the details in their head, who always walks in the users' shoes, who obsesses about making the UX a great experience, and who never backs down. Typically, this is the product manager. As the leader, you need to either play this role or build up the project manager, providing confidence and defending against popular opinion if it is contrary to the project manager's.

It is important to remember that as a design architect, you have a fixed capacity. Every time you say "yes" to one feature, you say "no" to many. You need to be as clear as possible about what audience you are building the product for and focus on that, even if it means you let go of other audiences. If you try to build a product that everyone can use, although some will use it, no one will love it and tell their friends about the product.

After you document the must-have features and experiences, remember that a product gains more by going deep rather than going wide. Our goal is to get lots of passionate users rather than many lukewarm users. The former begets more users, creating exponential (viral) growth, while the latter does not take us anywhere.

Once we know what to build, we need to break down the system among teams. Each team should have seven to nine people (two-pizza teams) and should be able to deploy their part of the system independently. This means that they should have their own code repository and control their own deployment pipeline. If a team grows beyond this size, we need to divide the team, the code repositories, and the deployment processes. By dividing the team, we embrace Conway's law, which states that organizations design systems that mirror their own communication structure rather than fighting it.[1]

The next step is to define the APIs exposed to the outside and the APIs provided and consumed by each team. As we discussed in Chapter 2, public APIs need careful planning, and all APIs need good UX. We should focus on this with all architects and team leads. It's vital that we document the system's component breakdown and communicate to the team the APIs in detail. After that, the rest of the design defines the finer semantics of the APIs and figures out their implementations. We should get the implementation team involved at this stage and empower them to come up with a design that the architects can review and help to improve.

Before starting work, we need to communicate and reiterate the user journey and its importance to the team. We must have enough UX skills at the ground level, always playing the devil's advocate: needling, questioning, and taking apart the UX. We must give the users a voice and make sure they are heard. One-third of Apple's team are UX designers, which may or may not be practical for you, but Apple clearly has its priorities right.

---

1. See https://en.wikipedia.org/wiki/Conway%27s_law

Find and celebrate (e.g., in a town hall meeting) creative UX designs that elevate the customer experience to new levels. Your QA and UX teams should question the first user experience of every feature, which often makes the difference between passionate versus lukewarm customers.

When possible, while shaping the overall design, we, the architects, should let the team design the detail for each part. It is said that a software architect should think like a gardener rather than like a commander. The former shapes, curates, and removes weed, whereas the latter defines and dictates. An architect should curate rather than dictate, shape rather than define, and incite discussion rather than labeling.

In the short term, dictating an architecture is faster and may even be cheaper. However, in the long run, we build better teams by letting team members think for themselves, letting them evolve the architecture, and sometimes, letting them make their own mistakes. When we focus on the team, they'll get better with time. Execution gets easier if the architecture is the team's idea in the first place.

As described in the seminal essay "The Use of Knowledge in Society" by Friedrich A. Hayek, the people who are closest to the actual system have the best context and are in the best place to make decisions in solving contextual problems such as design.[2] Therefore, it is best to design the top-level architecture with the key people: let architecture owners design services and let component developers design the components. However, this does not mean we cannot have consistent best practices. For example, one best practice could be to use the classical thread-per-request service implementation for services unless they become a critical bottleneck. Any subteam who would want to do differently needs to defend and justify their position.

If there are multiple teams, you will need architectural owners responsible for several logically related teams. Architectural owners should run design meetings and escalate topics for wider discussions as needed. They are also responsible for documenting the design and communicating it.

Note that it is not ideal to assemble everyone in all architecture meetings. Beyond seven to ten participants, the meetings lose their effectiveness. My recommendation is to do smaller meetings but take detailed notes, which can be edited by the architectural owners and shared with all developers. Also, any architecture discussion that can be done through writing (e.g., chats, shared documents, emails, and so forth) should be done as publicly as possible so that all developers can see it and understand its direction.

Make Decisions and Absorb Risks

As we discussed in Chapter 2, you must make decisions and absorb any uncertainty and risk. For example, Jeff Bezos's decision criteria in his Stakeholder letters can serve us well in this regard.[3]

---

2. https://www.econlib.org/library/Essays/hykKnw.html

3. For an analysis and a list of his Stakeholder letters, see https://www.cbinsights.com/research/report/bezos-amazon-shareholder-letters/.

You should delegate any decision that is not critical to the project's outcome. A decision is critical to the outcome when the outcome is significantly different between the best and most obvious solution, not when the money tag or the importance tag is high. Sometimes, architectural abstractions such as interfaces allow us to delay these decisions, but we *should* delegate any decision that is reversible without significant cost.

We are left with only critical and irreversible decisions, which should not be common. In such instances, we must have a sense of when the decision is needed. This can be when the team is running out of useful things to do or when a delay could affect delivery dates. Meanwhile, you can ask for more information, experiments, PoCs, and opinions. There is a point, however, where a decision is needed; a point where some decision is better than no decision. Jeff Bezos advises us to make that decision when we know 70% of the information because we almost never have all the information. This is a good rule of thumb; however, how to measure 70% in a mathematical sense is not made clear, and you need to use your intuition to detect 70%.

When deciding, we can handle uncertainty using the five questions and the seven principles we detailed in Chapter 2 and in Part III. When we arrive at the point of decision, we must make it, taking responsibility for whatever uncertainty is left. Then, we must communicate our decision directly without hiding behind any form of ambiguity or evading responsibility.

We must always consider '"not keeping anyone waiting due to absence of our decisions" as our operational goal'. An exception might be pertaining to critical and irreversible decisions; in this case, we should minimize any delay by starting our investigation process early.

Demand Excellence

You can't oversee everything. You could choose to focus your attention on hard problems, even micromanage them if they are important enough. Nevertheless, your direct impact is limited, and even with careful handling, the architecture ultimately descends to the level of your team, their understanding, their knowledge, their judgment, and their depth of thinking. We must demand excellence and get our teams to think deeply. There are several ways to do this.

First, ask probing questions that are designed for understanding and to get your team to think. Ask why; ask for the reasons for their choices; ask why not. Ask what if, and most importantly, ask how you know. Try to read between the lines and watch for what is not being said compared to what is being said.

For example, if a developer does not talk about the performance of a potentially performance-sensitive part, often it's because that piece has not been tested or the performance is not good. Most people do not like to share bad news. You need to sense this and draw it out. Do this in team meetings, but keep your comments respectful and never overreact, regardless of what you learn. Prompt others for opinions, tap into the expertise in the team, and use questions to establish different people as experts in different areas.

Questions also play a role in educating everyone. Questions are by far the most effective tool leaders have for shaping their team. For more information, the book *Ask More: The Power of Questions to Open Doors, Uncover Solutions, and Spark Change* by Frank Sesno (AMACOM, 2017) is a good reference.

The second way is to use checklists. Create checklists of questions that are useful for different situations and use them. Some of the checklist items should include showing the design to different people such as security experts, SRE architects, and UX experts, and then getting feedback to create discussion. With this last trick, you can make checklists work even in unclear situations. Atul Gawande's book, *The Checklist Manifesto* (Henry Holt and Company, 2009), has a great treatment on this subject.

The team needs to understand that they must find answers and not follow your instructions to the letter. When a new person joins my team, I tell them that it is their job to find answers and mine is to break those answers down until I can't break them anymore. It takes some time, with repetition on my part, to break the habit of looking to someone else for the answers, when it does sink in, they start to do much better work.

Tell your team that what they design is their responsibility, and if the architecture fails, the architect also fails in that instance. Be clear that all architecture fails in some way, but we must all learn from the failures. When something fails, probe until you understand in detail what happened and always end with a second-order question such as "What can we (notice it is *we*, not *you*) do to avoid this from happening in the future?" Then, make sure those decisions are followed. Moreover, if one of your judgments fails, admit it and use the same process. This prevents everyone from being defensive about their failures.

Use the idea of *gross negligence* to raise the bar. Gross negligence is, as per Wikipedia, a "lack of slight diligence or care" or "a conscious, voluntary act or omission in reckless disregard of a legal duty and of the consequences to another party."[4] When a mistake comes close to gross negligence, talk to the person involved one on one. Explain why that aspect is important and mutually decide how to avoid that problem in the future. Focus on the problem, not the person. Use a coaching style and let them come up with the answer or answers.[5] Do not overreact. Take things the team member can't control out of the equation because fear kills creativity.

An important part of deep thinking is connecting the dots across different parts of the system. Look out for these connections and proactively act to strengthen them (e.g., ask the teams to brainstorm about the topic) or to reduce potential problems (e.g., get the teams to agree on who does what and when). Nudge others to do the same. If you catch someone doing this work, express your appreciation for that in the next team meeting.

Paul Graham talks about a skill he calls *relentlessly resourceful*, which he defines as a bias to action and a knack for finding a way around walls.[6] This skill lets a team push until they reach

---

4. https://en.wikipedia.org/wiki/Gross_negligence

5. A good reference for a coaching style is Michael Bungay Stanier's book, *The Coaching Habit: Say Less, Ask More & Change the Way You Lead Forever* (page 2, 2016).

6. See Haroon Meer's blog at https://blog.thinkst.com/2022/08/always-be-hacking.html.

or exceed the bar. The same skills are closely associated with thinking deeply, in addition to a bias for action.

The way to achieve excellence is to show that it is important to you. You can do this by allocating time to understand and discuss what happens, learn how to avoid failures or problems, and follow up as needed. Show that it is important to you, that you will not relent, and the team will do their best.

Communicating the Design

Even the best architecture is useless unless well executed. To this end, we must communicate the architecture to the team. The goal is to convey the high-level architecture and the rationale behind the decisions to facilitate meaningful debate, not to make everyone understand all the details of the design.

Communicating the design is a difficult problem. I am not a believer in complicated UML diagrams and hundred-page reports. No one reads them without an enforcer with a stick. These types of items create resentment and waste valuable time. I have, however, seen the following approach work over the years.

We can describe the bigger picture using rough ad hoc diagrams (like I used in Chapter 2), one-to-two-page descriptions, and sequence diagrams for complex use cases. We do the same for each service, and we must update each document when the code changes. Developers do not universally understand the meaning (the semantics) of ad hoc diagrams. However, these diagrams provide flexibility when presenting information in a manner that is easy to understand.

We also need a small description that outlines the design with the ad hoc diagrams. Most importantly, we should document APIs and message formats in detail, creating the foundation for communication between subteams.

Also, weekly or biweekly architecture meetings and periodic talks are potent tools at our disposal. The former discusses and evolves the architecture, while the latter communicates the big picture. Team leads and senior engineers play a crucial role in communication in both events.

Evolving the System: How to Learn from Your Users and Improve the System

Sometimes, when we build a product, the need and market are already there. For example, if the government builds a system to issue vehicle revenue licenses, the need is clear. Many will use it, assuming it is not too hard.

However, many systems must compete with other alternatives in the open market. When we build a system, a key idea is a product-market fit: building the product the market wants and is willing to pay for. Often, we are not the only player; in this case, we need to compete and outperform the other side in at least some dimensions.

For years, dreaming up a system, building it, and taking it to the market were the norm. We can manage risk by talking to potential users before building the product, while building it, and after.

Even with such studies, there are lots of risks. For example, our users may not be representative, which can lead to significant surprises, and if there are noteworthy problems, we need to update the product. With the old model, the update cycle is long—years to months—so our products used to change slowly. However, armed with startup experience, we can sometimes do better.

A key theme of the book is to take an interactive approach, creating opportunities for us to learn from users, tweak the product, and make informed decisions. A key aspect of this approach is feedback. There are two primary ways to get feedback.

The first is to interview users and watch them in action if possible. Common practice is to ask them to record the screens, then interview them to understand the system more. It is well understood in UX research that asking users may be misleading; watching them in action is much more reliable.

The second is to build data collection into the product, ranging from data collected at key points and traces to full-screen recordings. If your product is offered as an SaaS, where you host and run the product, this step is easy. Otherwise, it is more complicated but often possible.

If we can get feedback and respond to the difference between user expectations and the system, then we have a much better chance of aligning well with the customers, faster than others, and ultimately winning them over. Furthermore, we have a better chance of keeping the customers by responding to evolving requirements.

I believe every architect should consider feedback-collecting systems as part of their design and use it to fine-tune the UX. This is true even for systems where users are already locked in, such as government systems, because a better UX provides better adoption and happy users, raising goodwill and even indirectly saving money (e.g., money spent on customer support and fixing user mistakes).

The second part to data collection is about how we can understand and respond to user feedback. This is an issue that has been widely discussed under the topic of *growth hacking* (sometimes also called product lead growth). I refer you to two books for details:

- *Design-Driven Growth: Strategy & Case Studies for Product Shapers* by Molly Norris Walker (self-published as an ebook or audio, 2018)

- *Hacking Growth: How Today's Fastest-Growing Companies Drive Breakout Success* by Sean Ellis and Morgan Brown (Currency, 2017)

Growth hacking is often used to make decisions in marketing, but as described in *Hacking Growth*, the same idea also is used successfully to improve products. Following are some of the key ideas and how they fit in with the product's architecture.

The key idea in growth hacking is to understand the user journey, asking what we want our successful users to do. Then, we should convert the user journey to funnels where advanced stages correspond to users who derive more value from the system. Finally, we optimize the product by optimizing the funnel. For example, Figure 13.1 shows a funnel where users can come, build applications, and run them in production.

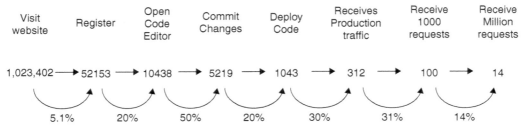

Figure 13.1
Example of a growth hacking funnel.

The top line in Figure 13.1 shows how users progress through the system to more and more valuable stages. The second line shows the conversion rates between stages in the funnel. Then, improvements in the system are reflected by progressing more users further down the funnel. We can explore where to improve the system to take more people down the funnel. There are two possible approaches.

First, we can compare current usage against a history and improve the funnel where conversion rates are weakest. Second, because some of the stages in the funnel are well defined (for example, the conversion rates from website to production, registrations to retained users, and retained users to customer conversion), we can compare our funnel to those well-known numbers and pick the place to optimize.

Let's say a typical SaaS conversion from website to registrations is 5%, so a 5.1% conversion is good. However, only 20% of the people who committed the code deployed it to production, which shows us what may need improvement. The next step is to identify potential reasons for fewer conversions and come up with solutions that we want to test. For example, there may be some UX problem that makes it hard for users to deploy their code.

When we find and choose the best solution, say, for users running the system on their own, we need to make and issue a new release, hoping that the users will pick up the new version soon. However, if we run the system as an SaaS, then we can update it immediately. We could do even better by running A/B tests to verify that the fix indeed works. A/B tests split the users among two versions of the product, typically between the version before the fix and the one after the fix, and measure the outcome (e.g., how many people become customers) to compare the two versions.

Hacking Growth by Sean Ellis and Morgan Brown discusses many such use cases. Fixes required to improve the funnel are often counterintuitive. Using A/B tests ensures that we only apply changes that have positive effects to keep improving the system.

The use of growth hacking provides three primary advantages. First, it lets us capture concrete feedback early, understand it in detail, and act on that feedback in a systematic manner, making the system responsive to the customers' needs. Second, with most systems, marketing is a significant expense, and growth hacking enables us to hold off significant spending for marketing until we know that we can meet user expectations and have a product market fit, which significantly improves our chances of success. Finally, growth hacking lets us tease out user opinions (e.g., by placing upcoming features as menu items early and then checking how many users are interested in the new features).

A successful growth hacking practice requires leaders to get several things right. First, the growth hacking team requires skills in UX, data science, and architecture, which is a tricky combination to find, so we need to plan for and build those skills. Second, more growth hacking experiments typically lead to better outcomes. However, running more experiments requires us to fix identified problems quickly and test them, which requires agility in system architecture, execution, and creativity also. Third, we can run many potential tests, ranging from shades of colors to major UX design choices, but we need to use data to pick and choose experiments that can provide big wins.

Leadership Considerations

Tech leaders should always pay attention to their relationship with the business that provides the funding for their project. The business has the right to be kept in the loop about the project's progress and to intervene if necessary.

Excellent tech leaders build trust with their boss and the rest of the business. You already have enough technical challenges; you don't need extra pressure from above. The second step to build trust is to understand and protect the company's interests. Communicate these interests and their impact on decisions to your team, explaining and answering any questions. Do this as often as needed. The third step is to speak the business language. Understand how the business operates, who the key customers are, and why processes are set up the way they are.

The final step is to understand that businesses hate surprises. Delivering a product late or going over budget is frowned upon. But if you deliver too early or cost less than expected, that also indicates their estimation and understanding of the team were incorrect.

No matter what you do, there will be surprises. The key is to communicate them early and explain the reasons. Don't overpromise or underpromise. Always keep the business informed. Good tech leaders are rare. If you're reasonable, represent business interests, deliver results, and keep your promises, the business will gladly let you do your thing. If they don't, you should be able to find a place that does.

When it comes to building the system, there are several uncertainties.

First, we can't know all user needs up front, and we can't foresee all architectural details. Some will emerge when coding, some after releasing the system. Our initial design might need to change as we gather more information.

Second, the business context, as identified by business architecture and the five questions from Chapter 2, can change. The best design evolves with the business context.

The leader's job is to manage uncertainty and provide clear goals for the team. The main tool to do this is a fast feedback cycle, enabling learning and necessary adjustments.

This chapter's main focus is on establishing a fast feedback cycle, removing anything that slows developers down from completing iterations, receiving feedback, and learning. Ensure developers can do their jobs efficiently. Get personally involved and solve issues that hold the developers back.

Once this system is set up, make decisions when the team finds it difficult, take responsibility, and give them a clear next goal. Learn from this process and repeat, always keeping the business context in mind.

The rest is about standard leadership: demanding excellence, coaching the team, being understanding without tolerating carelessness. Foster a learning environment.

Lastly, most projects fail not because leaders don't know what to do, but because it's hard to do the right thing consistently. Remember that, stick to basics, and do the work!

Good luck! Now go and make the world a better place by building better systems.

Summary

Following are key takeaways from this chapter:

- Most projects have a few basics wrong, incurring significant costs. Pay attention to the basics, get them right, and ensure continuity. Basics ensure developers do not have to jump through hoops to do their job. Developers are the most expensive resource you have. Put in place the right team and get out of the way.

- It is important that developers have an environment where they can easily test complicated scenarios.

- Quick fixes are important to create a better UX. Ensure large features do not slow down quick but important fixes. Neither program architects nor the product team should dictate the roadmap. Instead, watch and listen to the users. Understand what users are trying to do. Focus on understanding the user's journey and then ask this question: "How can we make it better?"

- You must make decisions and absorb any uncertainty and risk.

- Best way to achieve excellence is to show that it is important to you. Allocate time to understand and discuss what happens, learn how to avoid failures or problems, and follow up. Show that it is important to you, that you will not relent, and the team will do their best.

- Even the best architecture is useless unless well executed. Plan and communicate the architecture to the team.

- Use techniques like growth hacking to evolve the system using data-driven decisions.

- Business hates surprises either way. Communicate early and explain why. Do not overpromise or underpromise. Always keep the business up to date.

Index

B

Register Your Product at informit.com/register

Access additional benefits and save up to 65%* on your next purchase

- Automatically receive a coupon for 35% off books, eBooks, and web editions and 65% off video courses, valid for 30 days. Look for your code in your InformIT cart or the Manage Codes section of your account page.

- Download available product updates.

- Access bonus material if available.**

- Check the box to hear from us and receive exclusive offers on new editions and related products.

InformIT—The Trusted Technology Learning Source

InformIT is the online home of information technology brands at Pearson, the world's leading learning company. At informit.com, you can

- Shop our books, eBooks, and video training. Most eBooks are DRM-Free and include PDF and EPUB files.

- Take advantage of our special offers and promotions (informit.com/promotions).

- Sign up for special offers and content newsletter (informit.com/newsletters).

- Access thousands of free chapters and video lessons.

- Enjoy free ground shipping on U.S. orders.*

Offers subject to change.

** *Registration benefits vary by product. Benefits will be listed on your account page under Registered Products.*

Connect with InformIT—Visit informit.com/community

 Pearson

Addison-Wesley • Adobe Press • Cisco Press • Microsoft Press • Oracle Press • Peachpit Press • Pearson IT Certification • Que